Shakespeare's Other Language

RUTH NEVO

Methuen · New York and London

For Yani, Gideon, and Amos

First published in 1987 by
Methuen, Inc.
29 West 35th Street, New York
NY 10001

Published in Great Britain by
Methuen & Co. Ltd
11 New Fetter Lane, London
EC4P 4EE

© 1987 Ruth Nevo

Printed at the University Press,
Cambridge

Library of Congress Cataloging in
Publication Data

Nevo, Ruth.
    Shakespeare's other language.
    Bibliography: p.
    Includes index.
    1. Shakespeare, William, 1565–
    1616 – Tragicomedies.
    I. Title.
    PR2981.5.N48   1987   822.3'3
    87-11096

    ISBN 0 416 06402 7

British Library   Cataloguing   in
Publication Data

Nevo, Ruth
    Shakespeare's other language.
    1.   Shakespeare,   William   –
    Tragicomedies
    I. Title
    822.3'3   PR2981.5

    ISBN 0 416 06402 7

Contents

Acknowledgments

My greatest indebtedness for the writing of this book is to the graduate seminar of students and younger colleagues, especially Aviva Furedy, Elizabeth Freund, Josh Wilner, Ephraim Gerber, on whom I first tried it out. Without their enthusiastic interest and encouragement my version of Shakespeare's other language would probably be by now a dead language. Dr Esther Goshen, in that same seminar, was most helpful in contributing insights derived from her clinical experience, as was Dr Rifka Eifferman, who kindly read and criticized the *Pericles* chapter before it was given at a seminar on psychoanalysis and literature organized by Shlomith Rimmon-Kenan under the auspices of the Centre for Literary Studies of the Hebrew University. My best of critics, Hillel Daleski, read the entire manuscript with his customary scrupulous rigor and, gallantly putting aside his own gnawing doubts about the whole project's validity, saved me from many slips and excesses. Conversations and correspondence with Bennett Simon at an early stage and Stanley Cavell at a critical later stage of the work were quintessential, and invaluable.

My warmest thanks go too to Debbie Berman and Linda

Robinson, research assistants, who devoted themselves untiringly during a sabbatical year to saving me time and trouble, and to the Israel Academy of Sciences and Humanities for providing me with them.

Harold Jenkins and E. A. Honigmann invited me to give "Subtleties of the isle" at the triennial IAUPE conference at York in 1986. The chapter on *The Winter's Tale* received a first rough draft – which later proved to be the first draft of the whole – during an idyllic month's residence at the Study and Conference Center at Bellagio, in 1983. I am grateful to the Rockefeller Foundation for the generous provision of so fair a seedtime.

And deeply grateful, as ever, to Natan, for his unfailing support.

Finally, I want to thank Janice Price for her steadfast confidence in this book, and Sarah Pearsall for seeing it so speedily and efficiently through the press.

Ruth Nevo
The Hebrew University
Jerusalem

I have dreamt the world as you dreamt your work, my
Shakespeare, and among the forms of my dream are you,
who, like myself, are many and no one.

(Jorge Luis Borges, *Everything and Nothing*)

Tis still a dream, or else such stuff as madmen
Tongue and brain not; either both or nothing,
Or senseless speaking, or a speaking such
As sense cannot untie.

(William Shakespeare, *Cymbeline*)

Ellipsis and pleonasm, hyperbaton or syllepsis, repression,
repetition, apposition – these are the syntactical displacements, metaphor, catachresis, autonomasis, allegory,
metonymy, and synecdoche – these are the semantic
condensations in which Freud teaches us to read the
intentions – ostentatious or demonstrative, dissimulating or
persuasive, retaliatory or seductive – out of which the
subject modulates his oneiric discourse.

(Jaques Lacan, *Ecrits*)

1

Beyond genre

The subject of my study in the following pages will be the four later romances of Shakespeare which have notoriously presented critics with thorny problems both theoretical and interpretative. Indeed, no comprehensive theory exists to account for the form and character of these plays, nor any definitive nomenclature even with which to refer to them. Some of them have been acclaimed as among his most praised and prized productions, some – indeed all of them at some time or another – have been relegated to a distinctly lower, or even doubtful place in the canon.

"The 'problem' of the last plays," wrote Philip Edwards in a 1958 review of the criticism,

> may be stated quite simply. [They] form a group with similar characteristics, incidents and endings. They seem more closely related than any other group of Shakespeare's plays. What they have in common makes them startlingly different from the plays which go before them. They are, moreover, written at the close of the author's writing career. So there is something of a mystery to be solved. The mystery is all the more interesting because the change in character appears to

be a change away from the control and concentration which Shakespeare had achieved in the great tragedies. Construction and characterization seem to show not greater artistic maturity, but less. (1958, 1)

For my own part I do not find a "mystery" where Philip Edwards did. That a writer returns again and again to a theme when it constitutes for him unfinished business presents a problem only if one is interested in filling in gaps in an incomplete biography. In fact, Shakespeare is throughout the most reiterative of poets – his returns and recurrences are as incessant as they are exfoliating and diversified; his imagination kindles afresh to each redevelopment of familiar components, or, perhaps it would be truer to say, every work leaves in its wake a detritus of un- or not yet resolved or integrated components which leads on to the next.

"All Shakespeare's work from *Lear* to the end of his career," says Cyrus Hoy in a commanding statement of a commanding theme,

> seems to be generated by the tensions between two powerful imaginative efforts: on the one hand, to free the self from bondage to the kind of female monsters most horrifically embodied in Goneril and Regan, and on the other hand to replace the sense of female monstrosity with . . . an ideal of femininity on whom the imagination can bestow its tenderest sentiments, without the distractions of sexual desire. (1978, 81, 84)

This is indeed a theme to exercise an imagination, but why begin with *Lear*? What of *Titus Andronicus*, the sensational pathos of whose archaic father and abused and mutilated daughter reverberates behind all subsequent transformations of those figures? By the same token the farcical extravaganza of *The Comedy of Errors* contains the whole wandering romance story of vicissitude and family reunion which structures the later plays. The whole of the Shakespearean *opus* is a palimpsest – a mystic writing pad, to borrow Freud's famous exemplary toy – upon which are inscribed again and again re-presentations of lived experience in the forms of art.

What chiefly strikes us about these strange and interesting and beautiful plays if we attempt, as perhaps we should, to see them again as if for the first time, is their defiance of common sense. Their strangenesses, improbabilities, miraculous coincidences, anachronisms, divine interventions are so flagrant and often bizarre as to constitute a positive abdication of reason: decapitations – headless bodies and bodiless heads – persons buried at sea who survive, miraculously embalmed, a ravenous bear who devours grown men and leaves month-old babes untouched, innumerable shipwrecks, wondrously timely or wondrously untimely, an enchanted island, a magician, a magic storm, attendant spirits, a monster aborigine.

Yet what, in Shakespeare's non-historical fabrications, has been credible? We have become accustomed to think of his represented worlds as possible worlds, within reasonable fictional proximity to everyday, empirical reality. And up to a point this is so, where page-boy girls, for example, or bed-tricks, or fabulous cures are concerned. We accept the ghosts and witches of *Hamlet* and *Macbeth* as expressions of an historical belief in the supernatural, or we rationalize them as representations of hallucination, or conscience, and what follows these apparitions at the level of sheer event does no violence to our expectations of rational (even if perverse) motive and plausible occurrence in the represented worlds of court intrigue and murderous dynastic rivalry. Othello stories are daily newspaper fare, but even *Lear*, with all its wild excesses and its phantasmagoria, doesn't ask us, we feel, to take leave of our senses; and *A Midsummer Night's Dream*, which does, takes legitimate advantage of comic, and oneiric, licence for its manifestly preposterous fairies and fantasies. Yet, I submit, Shakespearean drama is throughout wilder than we have allowed ourselves to become accustomed to thinking. To the classicist purists of France its monstrous daughters and wives and villains, its fools and madmen, and above all its prodigious language have always seemed "gothic," barbarous, frenzied. "Shakespeare never sees things tranquilly," says Taine.

We are on the brink of an abyss; the eddying water dashes in headlong, devouring whatever objects it meets, bringing them to light again, if at all, transformed and mutilated. We pause stupified before these convulsive metaphors, which might have been written by a fevered hand in a night's delirium, which gather a pageful of ideas and pictures in half a sentence, which scorch the eyes they would enlighten. Words lose their sense, constructions are put out of joint . . . little concocted and incorrect phrases . . . by their irregularity, express the suddenness and the breaks of the inner sensation; trivial words, exaggerated figures . . . each is the extremity and issue of a complete mimic action; none is the expression and definition of a partial and limited idea. This is why Shakespeare is strange and powerful, obscure and original . . . the most immoderate of all violators of language . . . the furthest removed from regular logic and classical reason. ((1863) 1871, 309)

We cannot but feel the force of this characterization and it must surely prompt us to reflect upon the reasons for the taming, in our perception, of the wildness of Shakespeare. We no longer expurgate or rewrite him, but we naturalize him; our rationalist traditions cause us to make his drama, in both the academy and the theater, conformable to the demands of a sweet reasonableness. I believe that what has made this domestication possible is the firm generic architectonic of most of the plays. Through repeated experimentation Shakespeare evolved a form of comedy and a form of tragedy which, however distinctively his own, was based upon classical precept and example. The whole of Shakespeare's drama is riddled by the contrary and entangled urgencies of dread and desire, but the former is characteristically realized in tragic catastrophe, the latter in the eudaemonic resolutions of comedy, each, in its own way, containing and controlling the adversary elements within them. Ultimately it is to the fact of mortality that both the genres respond. Tragedy faces the terror of death but attempts to master it by extracting value from the tragic protagonist's progress to catastrophe via self-recognition and individuation – he dies in his own way. Comedy evades, circumvents or defers death through its matings and marriages, or represents mock deaths, or symbolic or illusory deaths which are triumphantly overcome.

So imperative a mental construct was the classical dualism of genre – toward death or toward love – that virtually the whole of innovative modern drama (from Chekhov to the Absurd) was required to dislodge or deconstruct it. "When I write a tragedy, I make them laugh, when I write a comedy I make them cry," said Ionesco. In the later plays, where Shakespeare's imagination plays upon his themes in a particular, and a particularly puzzling fashion, something of this contrary phenomenon already comes into view. The romances thwart or baffle the rational ordering and controlling forms of tragedy and comedy and thus become classifiable as tragicomedies – a mode of drama which became increasingly popular in the English theater after the turn of the century. The paradoxical term, a taxonomic scandal, itself requires investigation.[1] The anomalous, self-contradictory, mixed genre of these plays, or the mixing of genres within them – the analogy it becomes possible to descry, as it turns out, between the mode of tragicomedy and the state, or work, of mourning – forms one part of the inquiry I wish to conduct. The argument will necessarily be recursive for these are the very plays which will tell us what we can mean by the class tragicomedy. They are chief among the stock of texts to which the term must apply if it is to have any descriptive or taxonomic force at all.

Not that there were no precedents for mixings among Shakespeare's earlier plays: the disrupted comedy of *Love's Labour's Lost*, the scapegoat-dependent *Merchant of Venice* and the so-called "problem" comedies, *All's Well* and *Measure for Measure* all share with the romances their doubtful status. The "problem comedies" juggle with disturbing fears of extinction (male fears about being tricked in bed) and with bed-tricks that are counterphobic and benign. The *Merchant* employs law-tricks instead of bed-tricks for a similar purpose. The earlier *Love's Labour's Lost*, on the other hand, truncates its betrothal ceremonies with news of a father's demise, and challenges its protagonist to "move wild laughter in the throat of death" (V.ii.863). In these precursor tragicomedies,[2] as in the romances, either the differential relationship between tragic and comic components – between Thanatos and Eros – disturbs conventional, generic expectations of catharsis or resolution and invites response of a different kind, or they are drastically split between tragedy and comedy; *Measure for Measure*, for instance, right in the middle of its most highly explosive scene, with a grinding change of gear; and *The Winter's Tale* equally so, though with the gentler mediation of Father Time. In terms of the established syntax of tragedy and comedy these tragicomedies are not well-formed sentences. They are ungrammatical. It is this dismantling of established disposition which thrusts into prominence those aspects of the presentation which strike us so compellingly as nonsensical, inconsequential, ridiculous or fantastic, though matters perhaps no less surrealistic in more generically manageable plays we have, so to speak, taken in our stride. Deprived of the support of generic intelligibility we need to fashion other ground rules to construe them, to make sense of what doesn't, on the face of it, make sense. In these later plays, Shakespeare, like late Yeats, like late Picasso, yields to his themes, loosens or even abandons the constraints of classical category and moves beyond genre towards an indeterminate mode akin to reverie.

As does also late Freud. There is a strange affinity between these strangely anguished "comedies" and Freud's late review of his own theories. Freud's *Beyond the Pleasure Principle* is itself an essay in deconstruction. Both the biological instincts he says are conservative, both seek homeostasis, that is, death. The paper is a melancholy disquisition, Freud's displaced mourning for his daughter, an oceanic death-wish fantasy; a tragicomedy. Shakespeare's tragicomedies are also essays beyond the pleasure principle and toward mourning. They are structured neither upon the masculine irresolvable either/or bind of tragedy, which makes disaster inevitable, nor upon the harmonizing feminine both/and of the comedies, which conjure resolution out of a wise folly, but upon an irreducible indeterminacy of gain and loss, loss and restitution. They evade, or transcend the controlling modes in a two-term compromise formation which allows for the expression of both, counterpointing death and love, threat and hope, desire and dread, dream and nightmare.

Yet, if we are either stunned, or anesthetized, by what might sometimes seem an unsophisticated assault upon our credulity in the phantasmagoria of the late plays, we are also decoyed and seduced (as we have always been) by the incomparable realism of Shakespearean characterization and dialogue, into taking these absurd fabrications seriously.

How do we, how have we taken them – "mouldy old tale[s]/Like *Pericles*" as Ben Jonson in an acerbic moment called them[3] – seriously? The fantastic is a literary category of great antiquity and popularity,[4] but the fact of the matter is that critics have been greatly bothered by this mode of the Shakespearean fantastic with its peculiar mixture of the mimetic and the unreal. Philip Edwards expresses a common view mildly when he says, "construction and characterization seem to show not greater artistic maturity but less" (1958, 1). Severer strictures have been made. All of the plays have been called "crude," "incoherent," "ill-made," "naive," "careless" or simply "silly." Either the dramatist was "getting bored," as Strachey (1922, 60) notoriously held, or was "tortured by a sense of inexpressiveness and failure" (James, 1937, 207). R.J. Kaufman, in a review article called "Puzzling Epiphanies," takes a bold, adversary step: "Precisely the challenge to the attentive critic of these remarkable productions," he says, " – what is most exciting about them – is their bold abdication of the securities of [the] articulate decorum ... which is the Shakespearean achievement. They demand ... more active participation, more mind, a wider repertoire of existent feelings in the spectator" (1963, 402). This is a banner under which I am happy to do battle, for it is indeed to the pursuit of "the more active participation," the "mind" and the "repertoire of feelings" demanded by the plays, that the following studies will be devoted, though not by way of the main methods of recuperation whereby criticism has traditionally risen to their challenge.

One such method has been to identify folklore or fairy-tale motifs, appropriate to the mode of romance,[5] to account for the weirdness of the invented events. These are then, in effect, set aside while attention is given to the wit and wisdom of a great humanist culture and the incomparable high mimetic art which are inscribed everywhere in the text. Another has been to interpret allegorically, and a variety of ingenious anagogical themes, mythological, philosophical, theological, have been energetically advanced to sweeten the irrational pill and ease the strain the plays' implausibilities make upon our powers to suspend disbelief.[6] Perhaps we should not allow ourselves to be thus diverted by extrapolated conceptual schemes, however inventive and ingenious. Perhaps what we should take seriously is precisely the raw, the odd, the counterrational in them, regarding these as possible outcroppings of a not immediately visible significance, rather than allowing their improbabilities to become familiar to us as a scaffolding, somewhat antiquated, for the lyric loveliness of the winds of March or cloud-capped towers, or the grander themes of deliverance and forgiveness. Fairy tales themselves, if that is what they are, have been taken seriously by inquiring minds – Bruno Bettelheim's study (1976) is well known – to excellent effect. I suggest that we should neither institutionalize them as repositories of traditional ethical and philosophical themes nor relegate them to a backwater of the Shakespearean canon – an honorable exception being made, always, for the valedictory *The Tempest* with its unabashed enchantments. I believe that if they are to speak to us, to our modern temperament and our modern insight, if they are to move us and to become vital to us, their familiarities must become strange and their strangenesses familiar in a new way. It is an investigation into the uncanny that we must undertake. My own attempt at a reading of these plays will therefore invoke the findings and methods of present-day post-psychoanalytic semiotics, which finds in rifts at the realist–rational level of plot, character and diction evidence of unconscious signification, of the language of dream and fantasy. It is the interplay of that other language with the manifest events and dialogue which may yield the new insights we seek.

Philip Edwards averred that we have not yet learned "a critical language capable of interpreting the Romances" (1958, 18), but such a language does already exist. What Jacob Arlow has called a "syntax of unconscious fantasy" (1979, 380) has, indeed, existed for nearly a century, during which period it has, itself ramifying and developing, entered into various alliances and conflicts with the languages of literary criticism. It has in recent years reemerged upon the literary horizon in particularly fruitful ways.

> Suppose I have a picture-puzzle, a rebus, in front of me. It depicts a house with a boat on its roof, a single letter of the alphabet, the figure of a running man whose head has been conjured away, and so on. Now I might be misled into raising objections and declaring that the picture as a whole and its component parts are nonsensical. A boat has no business to be on the roof of a house, and the headless man cannot run [etc.] . . . . But obviously we can only form a proper judgement of the rebus if we put aside criticisms such as these of the whole composition and its parts and if, instead, we try to replace each separate element by a syllable or word that can be represented by that element in some way or other. The words which are put together in this way are no longer nonsensical but may form a poetical phrase of the greatest beauty and significance. A dream is a picture puzzle of this sort.

The quotation will no doubt be recognized. It comes from Freud's *The Interpretation of Dreams* (1900, 277–8) which, together with *The Psychopathology of Everyday Life* and *Jokes and their Relation to the Unconscious* constitutes a triad of possibly the most seminally important books for the study of language and literature to have been produced in this century. Their effects have been incalculable, upon literature, upon culture, upon our ways of thinking, upon our entire civilization; but let me make it quite clear that I refer to what Geoffrey Hartman has called "The Interpretor's Freud"[7] rather than what one might call The Clinician's Freud, which is another matter altogether, although certain moves that have been made recently from the therapist's side towards the literary critic's, have stressed, again, the commonalty of the terrain shared by both, especially the narrative terrain.[8] Both analysts and literary critics deal with stories about people, constructed and told, in both cases, with a considerable degree of fictionality, and entailing, in both cases, reflection upon the very notion of person. Those that the critics deal with can't answer back however. Nor can they provide ongoing additional information to assist us in our exegeses. This is a cardinal difference (of which Ernest Jones' (1955) character analysis of Hamlet made us all paradoxically the more aware) and it should surely never be forgotten; but when we hear a practicing psychoanalyst speaking of his exegetic task we must be struck by a resemblance to the practice of the literary critic. The analyst's listening, Dr Arlow tells us, must be

> exquisitely sensitized to the various aspects of the patient's speech, to what is being said, to how it is being said, when and in what context it is being said, to what is not said . . . not only to the emotional tone . . . but also to the figurative constellations employed in his language. (1979, 366)

Another practicing psychoanalyst has talked of the importance of "the unsaid . . . that lies in the holes of the discourse" (Lacan, 1977, 93) – a picturesque way of referring to what literary critics have long called "suggestion" – and pointed out that the words "transference" and "metaphor" have identical roots in Latin and Greek respectively. These are new emphases, the older connection between the domain of the written and the lived having been located, not in the forms, modes and functions of narrative fiction, nor in the displacements of signifiers, but in the figural or thematic *content* of symbols and myths.

The analogies between the two kinds of analysis, the psychological and the literary – as between their fields of study – have been evident from the beginning. Yet curiously enough, the relations between the practice of psychoanalytic interpretation and the practice of literary interpretation has been marked throughout the psychoanalytic era by a persistent ambivalence. There has been between the two disciplines a mutual hunger to partake of each other's knowledge. "We laymen," wrote Freud in 1908,

> have always been intensely curious to know . . . from what sources that strange being, the creative writer, draws his material, and how he manages to make such an impression on us with it and to arouse in us emotions of which, perhaps, we had not even thought ourselves capable. (1908, 143)

Conversely, Lionel Trilling in 1951 announced unequivocally:

> The Freudian psychology is the only systematic account of the human mind which, in point of subtlety and complexity, of interest and tragic power, deserves to stand beside the chaotic mass of psychological insights which literature has accumulated through the centuries. . . . the human nature of the Freudian psychology is exactly the stuff upon which the poet has always exercised his art. (1951, 34)

Yet there has been a reciprocal hostility too; alliance and conflict have alternated, as between rival twins, competitors for the right to analyze. Despite the large number of psychoanalytic interpretations of individual plays, there has been little concerted effort to use Freud's "systematic account of the human mind" as a legitimate tool in Shakespearean studies, and sustained attempts at what one might call a psychocritical synthesis between analytic discoveries and mainline critical wisdom are still few and far between.[9] The course of mutually fructifying, unstable and volatile relations between the two contenders for hermeneutic primacy is itself a fascinating chapter in the history of ideas, to which figures from both camps like Ernest Jones (the first of whose many revisions of *Hamlet and Oedipus* was published in 1923), Simon Lesser (1957), Ernst Kris (whose *Psychoanalytic Explorations in Art*, co-authored with E.H. Gombrich, appeared in 1964), Norman Holland (whose psychoanalytical–literary critical enterprise began in 1964), Jacques Lacan ([1966] 1977), Anton Ehrenzweig

(1967), Paul Ricoeur (1970; 1974), Harold Bloom (1975; 1976), Geoffrey Hartman (1978), Shoshana Felman (1978; 1980), André Green (1979; 1985), Julia Kristeva (1980), and Meredith Skura (1980; 1981), among many others, have greatly contributed. This history cannot be my concern here; Norman Holland (1976), Alan Roland (1978), and more recently, Elizabeth Wright (1984) and Francis Baudry (1984) have provided us with comprehensive overviews.[10] But before I offer in the following studies the results of my own immersion in these inebriating streams, certain clarifications are called for.

A great deal is needed to transform Freud's rhetoric of the dream-work – condensation, displacement (translatable, Lacan found, as metaphor and metonymy respectively (1977, 156–61)), image-making and secondary elaboration – into a basis for an oneiric reading of plays, or of any literary text. A drama is not a dream. As Ricoeur notes (1974), dream interpretation leads from a less intelligible meaning to a more intelligible meaning, and the same does not hold for literary texts, which, by virtue of their own immensely articulated, ratiocinated, shaped and patterned secondary elaborations, have intelligible meanings in the first instance. A drama is not even the narrative of a dream. And even the narrative of a dream – a told dream – is not a dream. As Meredith Skura points out:

> The primitive surface may indicate that the dreamer has actually gone back to a primitive way of seeing and representing the world . . . a mode of thinking in which we had not yet sorted out wish [or fear] from reality. . . . [but] the wakened dreamer looking at his own dream straddles the two worlds of remembered dream and waking consciousness, and for him there is always a play between two different ways of reading the dream. (1980, 356, 358)

This distinction between originary *wish* and original *mode* of representation, and the notion of an interplay between the two, and between either one and its later, more mature, judgemental, intellectual or verbal derivatives is very important; it can save us from the reductiveness endemic in regressivist Freudian readings and, in the refinements and complexities of practice, provide us with a new way "to implicate psychoanalysis in literature" (Felman, 1980, 145–6).

Robert Rogers has provided two useful books which help to make Freud's dream interpretation available for literary critics. One offers a psychoanalytic view of metaphor (1978), and the other of the double in literature (1970). One derives from Freud's account of the "Two Principles of Mental Functioning" (1911), the other from his unfinished, posthumously published paper on "The Splitting of the Ego in the Process of Defence" (1938). Both are essential reading for the project I have in mind in these studies, rich in exemplification and in detailed and valuable discussions of poems, plays and novels. Rogers describes the "two principles of mental functioning" isolated by Freud as the primary and secondary processes. The former, prior to the latter in human development, is spontaneous, "streamy," kaleidoscopic, associative, pictorial, "magical," seemingly random or inadvertent, unaffected by the constraints of logical consistency with its laws of non-contradiction or excluded middles, or by any requirement to distinguish between persons, places and times. There was no clock in the forest of Arden, it will be recalled, and there is no time in primary process. Places and bodies can be proxies for each other and personae can be split parts of a single whole, or several personages condensed into one. "The primary process," Rogers says, "pays no heed to common sense. That is one of its secret sources of power. It can equate almost anything with anything else even where the most rudimentary similarity exists" (1978, 17), and according to the primary process the signifier "equals reality," is "literally" as we say, what it represents or displaces. The secondary process is capable of abstraction, is analytical, conceptual, empirical, responsive to the external world and subject to the sorting out, problem-solving and reality-testing devices employed by the ego in its dealings with that world. As Freud pointed out, there is secondary revision already at work in the *narrative* of a dream – some shaping and ordering, some story-making, some symbolic interpretation – imposing itself upon the dream material. Conversely, Anton Ehrenzweig has insisted that the infantile primary process mentation is not necessarily simply archaic, primitive or regressive as Kris in *Psychological Explorations in Art* (1964) maintained, but valuable in its potential for greater integration if the two processes are not disassociated, but the channels of communication between them kept flexibly open. "The classical concept of the primary process (which forms unconscious phantasy)," Ehrenzweig says,

> denies it any structure. Unconscious phantasy does not distinguish between opposites, fails to articulate space and time as we know it, and allows all firm boundaries to melt in a free chaotic mingling of forms. Art, on the other hand, appears the embodiment of rigorous organisation. So it has been assumed that art's structure is exclusively shaped by conscious and preconscious functions, the so-called secondary process. But this will not do . . . . In the solution of complex tasks the undifferentiation of unconscious vision turns into an instrument of rigorous precision and leads to results that are fully acceptable to conscious rationality. (1967, 3–4)

Moreover, as Noy has argued (1979), primary process itself becomes developed, richer and more diversified; it is not (unless severely repressed) simply discarded or outgrown as the child matures but *accompanies* the acquisition of secondary process thought. This position rescues primary process for art, since it enables us to conceive of a continuum between the preverbal, syncretistic primary processes of the very young child's bodily or body-need fantasies and mature versions or derivatives of these in the adult.

As an exemplary instance of the primary and secondary processes in poetry, Rogers offers an analysis of a "sad saga" familiar in every English nursery. In "Three Blind Mice" he discovers a precipitate of a fantasy rooted in deep-seated castration anxiety which the song "succeeds . . . in generating, controlling, and dispelling" (1978, 20). "The theme of vision and blindness as symbolic lust and castration continues from the first line, through the repeated imperative 'see' in the second, to the emphasis on seeing an unusual sight in the penultimate line." Crime follows punishment, but "the stress on seeing . . . reassur[es] the detached listener that since he can see . . . he is himself whole and hale" (20). Freud's observation that fear of the loss of the phallus is often represented by a multiplication of the object which represents it helps to account for the three mice, themselves whole bodies for parts.

Rogers chooses a nursery rhyme for his exemplary interpretation because, "closer to sheer fantasy [it] reveal[s] the primary process in a relatively unadulterated way" (19). We at once encounter a distributive problem. Primary process in nursery rhymes may be "relatively" unadulterated, but secondary process, in the form of formal choices and compositional design – rhyme, rhythm and lexis – is also "relatively" highly elaborated. As he points out, the three beat rhythm duplicates the triad of mice, and form itself functions as defence: "the song is a round, something continuous, that does not get cut off in the end" (20). Rogers proposes the notion of "modal ambiguity" to account for and describe the infinitely varied and complex fluctuations, tensions and shifts between the two modes in literature, "the way the two modalites function in concert" (37), or are orchestrated. In this view I.A. Richards' observation (enunciated without benefit of psychoanalysis) regarding figurative discourse, "To read aright we need to shift with an at present indescribable adroitness and celerity from one mode to another" (1968, 193), becomes doubly pertinent. In *The Double in Literature* (1970) Rogers is able to indicate a modulation between an involuntary, defensive, unconscious splitting – defence by projection or disavowal – whereby disunited parts of the mind of a single individual are represented in separate personifications, and highly conscious literary treatments of *alter egos* and *doppelgängers*. He distinguishes two other modalities: a subterranean doubling as of "secret sharers," which is not manifestly overt at the surface level of the story and, conversely, the flamboyant "baroque" doubling which is to be found in certain modernist fiction of the self-reflexive or *mise-en-abyme* variety, "at once more ambiguous and more self-conscious" than the other kinds. Of doubling and splitting – decomposition, in psychoanalytical terminology – the following studies will have much to say. A moment's reflection will suggest how fertile a field for the observation of such personified condensations and displacements Shakespeare's symmetries and oppositions among characters provide. "Whenever decomposition takes place in narrative," Rogers notes, "the cast of characters is never as large as it would appear to be" (1970, 63).

Rogers' models are more satisfactory, because less rigidly dualistic than the bipolarity presented by Norman Holland in *The Dynamics of Literary Response* (1968), as also in his later reader-response revisions of his theory. Holland does speak of a continuum from infantile response to intellectual "significance," and is forcefully persuasive on the necessity, in the dynamics of literary response, of unconscious as well as conscious participation by the reader, but he also speaks quite regularly of "*translating* the traditional terms of humane thought into their emotional roots" (1964, 349, my italics). His dualism appears more clearly in the earlier statement: "It is a necessary condition for tragedy," he says, in *Psychoanalysis and Shakespeare* (1964), "that the defence it embodies fail, leading to punishment for an impulse towards pleasure; it is a necessary condition for comedy that it build up a defence, leading to gratification without punishment for an impulse towards pleasure" (338–9). For Norman Holland it is the dynamic interplay between the forces of repression and that which is repressed – wish versus censor – which accounts for the distortions, displacements, condensations – the compromise formations – whereby the dream, or poem, finds ways of having its cake and eating it, of revealing and concealing its burden of emotion, but his opposing of defence to fantasy – form as defence, fantasy as content – is regressive for literary criticism which has with much endeavour emancipated itself from that very crippling dichotomy. Just as for sophisticated criticism form *is* content, content form, so defence is, or may be, as much fantasy as fantasy is, or may be, defence. This has come to be acknowledged by psychoanalytic theory "of the third phase" – Holland's own term – and, to some extent, by

Holland himself: "By the third phase, I mean a psychoanalysis that has gone beyond the polarities of conscious/unconscious and ego/nonego to a psychology of self and other."[11] This later development in Holland's thinking is in line with the Kohutian extension of interest in the benign development of the self out of the primary narcissism of the infant,[12] and with Meredith Skura's recent account, in *The Literary Use of the Psychoanalytic Process* (1981), of the psychic function of fantasy.

It is exactly the notion of fantasy (the status of which, in *The Interpretation of Dreams*, Freud was as yet uncertain (1900, 632–4)) which we need to supplement a dualistic Freudian account of primary process in literature. Fantasies are already structured, Freud tells us, and can appear in dream as part of the dream façade or in daydreams, which are quite consciously articulated. Freud himself, however, tended to confine fantasy, wishful or aggressive, to the domain of the deprivations, frustrations and conflicts of the psychosexual stages of development in early infancy or childhood, which have undergone repression and "have become pre-historic" (346). For this reason his theory of literary creativity remained impoverished: art produces its formal blandishments as a mask for or distraction from the primal fantasies verbally or imagistically evoked; the camouflage provides cover under which the reader can similarly indulge and so defuse those fantasies, inevitably shameful or guilt-producing, according to the Freudian "school of suspicion" (Ricoeur, 1970, 33), in a socially acceptable way.

Meredith Skura has given a more satisfactory account of the function of fantasy in literature in the light of developments since Freud. So far from indicating autistic withdrawal from reality, fantasy is an essential means, not only for the productions of the creative imagination, but for the emergence of the human infant as it grows from within the initial nondifferentiation of baby and mother, into a capacity for mature object-relations between a self and a world. Artist and adult both, ideally, command the faculties of secondary revision, and are in viable intercommunication with their own forgotten, but nevertheless vital and continuingly active past.

It is the convergence of these faculties that produces, not only mature human beings, but the greatly moving works of art, which set into activity the whole soul of humankind, pleasing, unifying, clarifying, organizing, both at the level of conscious control – plan, symmetry, design, balance – and at the level of archaic resonance. The literary model is that of a processing of symbolic elements and of episodes into ordered and coherent narratives, possessing purposive characters and consequential occurrences, beginnings, middles and teleological ends, but which are also capable of evoking the tremors, in consciousness, of unconscious pressures and desires enmeshed in a network of tentacular roots, in Eliot's phrase. We impoverish our readings if we are not aware of the unconscious, the kinetic, the potentially chaotic, in the high energy discourse of literature, as much as we impoverish readings by ignoring cultural contexts. The rhythm of creativity swings between differentiated and undifferentiated levels of response; it is their co-operation rather than, or at least as well as, their antagonism that our work of transactive interpretation must discern. Neither undertones nor overtones can be dispensed with in this work; and neither can be easily or simply located in a single consciousness.

"The true building blocks of the imagination," says Skura,

> are not dreams, or daydreams but primitive fantasies. These are shaped not by wishes alone, but by all aspects of early experience . . . unlike wishes they are not an alternative to rational thinking but a primitive form of thinking – or of organising internal and external experience. (1981, 78)

With a significant change of metaphor from the artefactual to the organic she suggests the model of a branching tree as a means for comprehending the stratification of fantasies from different stages of maturation.[13] Merely to name a fantasy is as reductive as the well-known parlour game of Hunting the Phallic Symbol, for "the same" fantasy may take a very different form in an infant, an adolescent and an adult. We are able to identify a primitive oral fantasy in a scene of oceanic longing, or of transcendental bliss, or of fearful engulfment, as well as in derivatives such as the "pallid approximations" of "our adult thirsts and quenchings" (82), but "finding a derivative from the very top of the tree – for example, Paul mourning for his mother in *Sons and Lovers* or Stephen refusing to mourn for his in *Ulysses* – is very different from finding one sent out directly on a lower branch . . . as in Poe's story of A. Gordon Pym tormented by thirst in the midst of a threatening sea" (83).

Skura's account, though open to correction in the matter of Stephen's "refusing to mourn" for his mother (he has done, it would seem, little else in nearly a year), is salutary in its reminder that "the matter of Oedipus can be as varied a category as the matter of Troy" (81) and that interpretation is not "simply a matter of going back to progressively more fecaloid materials or of substituting the original breast for a beer" (81). What she calls "lower branch symbolism" in literature (Marlow's exploration of "a vast, fecund continent" in Conrad's *Heart of Darkness* is her example) is not "hiding a fantasy," but "bringing a dead metaphor to life" (86). The image expresses the thought rather than disguising it. "What makes literature special," she says, "is the way it draws upon fantasies and yet escapes from the chaos of pure fantasy. . . . What makes literature unique is . . . the play between kaleidoscopic patterns of fantasies on the one hand, and, on the other, the impression we get of a stabler action which emerges from it" (98–9).

The interpretation of fantasy in literature is peculiarly problematic. In fantasy identities merge and switch, eating and being eaten, loving and hating, wishes and fears, repeating and undoing, inner and outer, sons and fathers, mothers and daughters, murder and suicide are indiscriminate and interchangeable. "The French psychoanalysts' emphasis on repetition as the primal motive in fantasy, rather than wish-fulfilment" is fruitful, Skura suggests, but "it does not capture the sense of a kaleidoscopic recycling of partial, inverted and contradictory forms of fantasy" (96). What is missing, she feels, in the "French Freud" emphasis, is the identification of a controlling fantasy.

But the very notion of a "controlling" fantasy is also problematic. Holland places "control" in the ego-system of defences. Fantasy is for him the unruly repressed which the patterns and devices of form "manage" and "master." Formal "strategies" and "manoevres" allow for a monitored and regulatory gratification of deep-level fantasies. How in this view can a fantasy control? Like any dichotomy this one will bounce us back and forth as upon the horns of a dilemma even if we modify the notion of a controlling fantasy and think rather of a fantasy-in-the-making as being that which is embodied in the work. Consider Freud's image of the flawed crystal. "If we throw a crystal to the floor, it breaks; but not into haphazard pieces. It comes apart along its lines of cleavage into fragments whose boundaries, though they were invisible, were predetermined by the crystal's structure" (1932, 90). This is the obverse of another petrifactive metaphor Freud had also used: a dream, he says, "is as a rule like a piece of breccia, composed of various fragments of rock held together by a binding medium, so that the designs that appear on it do not belong to the original rocks embedded in it" (1915–16, 181–2). It is the intentionality of the "flaw" that is at stake in the contradiction between these two metaphors. What can we make of an unbroken crystal, or an unfragmented rock? "In what sense," asks David J. Gordon (1980, 183) "is an unconscious process evident within a highly integrated verbal field?" His answer is: "A text (like a patient) can only lead us to an intuition of a repressed idea when its coherence is flawed in a certain way, when, that is, its incoherence can be traced to inappropriately charged effects rather than to mere ineptness." But what is inept? Is parapraxis inept? Or is it rather the device of a crafty libido in whose grip the speaker is a helpless and passive tool? Freud's own rhetoric tends to shunt purposiveness onto the uncontrolled and indestructible forces of the psyche, or upon the "mechanisms" of cathexis, against which only a limited defence on the part of the ego is possible (see *Dreams*, 1900, 746, 775). He speaks of the dream (or the neurosis), as the subject of the discourse. Dreams "pick up" trivialities from the day's events; dreams cunningly "distort," "evade" censorship, "find" pictorial images to represent complex and ambivalent dream thoughts; "get control" of unfulfilled, instinctual, infantile wishes or memory traces, "condense," "displace," "transfer" intensities from objectionable to indifferent objects, etc. It is necessary (today!) to recall that Freud's professional orientation was, after all, that of the physician. Though he stressed the continuity of the normal with the neurotic, his objective was the healing of personalities inundated or overwhelmed by the primary processes, fixated upon primitive levels of functioning, and so doomed to repeat infantile symbolizations, splits and disassociations as symptoms. The diagnosis and relief of symptoms cannot provide a model for literary criticism.

If we are to use the Freudian discoveries fruitfully in our interpretations of literature we must be very clear that we are dealing with an analogy and not an identity. The analogy between the two analytic processes is inadvertently brought out by Ernst Kris in his discussion of "the good analytic hour" in "On Some Vicissitudes of Insight in Psycho-analysis" (1956). "The analytic process," he says, "with its inexhaustible complexities and vicissitudes is the core of psycho-analysis, of its therapeutic effectiveness and *its investigative value*" (445, my italics). The "good analytic hour" is characterized, Kris explains, by a sudden "convergence" of associations, dreams, memories, reported experiences, interpretations (of analysand and analyst), a coming together "of new elements . . . which seem familiar, so well do they fit into the scheme of things." He describes the feeling of the good analytic hour as "a beginning to make sense," a "lifting of a veil" over some meaning which had been subliminally perceived but to which one had previously been blind. This "'tuning in' . . . leads to the experience on which analytic therapy in its ideal case rests, to the experience of *insight*, in which the cognitive elements are merged with a particular kind of assurance" (448). No literary critic can read these words without an experience of *déjà vu*. We have all been there, and these have been our "good analytic hours" with our texts; but we do not always know that we have, we do not always encourage ourselves to approach texts in quite this way, and we have not for the most part adopted into our conscious intellectual repertoire the procedures which make such fruitful analyses possible.

A small example will make my point. In a 1976 survey of the criticism of Shakespeare's romances, David Hoeniger praises a discovery of "fresh echoes" by Northrop Frye: Autolycus' pretence that his shoulder bone is out and Antigonus' genuinely bear-devoured shoulder bone. "This is entertaining," he says, "but did the echo result from conscious design or quirks of Shakespeare's imagination?" (7). No one can study the Dream book or the case histories without realizing that it is the overlooked detail, the marginal, the trifling or the trivial, that is, more often than not, the prime precipitator of the analyst's findings, of Kris' "insight." Or that it is precisely the stumbling block to coherence that can suddenly be perceived to be the keystone of a new, more comprehensive configuration. "A true artist will agree with the psychoanalyst that nothing can be deemed insignificant or accidental in a product of the human spirit," says Ehrenzweig (1967, 21). Only the usual evaluation has to be reversed if a blind determinism of the instinctual drive is to be avoided. "Quirks" of the imagination are exactly what our free-floating attention should be alert to catching, for these, whether in the form of parapraxes, or the compromise formations of metaphor and other tropes, or repetitions and over-emphases, or evasions, silences, absences, syntactic transgressions, ellipses, or puns, catachreses, metatheses – involuntary or by way of witty word-play – are the ruses whereby the unconscious, that which is blocked from view but ceaselessly active, reaches consciousness. "Literature," says Eagleton, "does not exactly say what it means or mean what it says . . . It is not quite identical with itself" (1978, 182). In the discontinuity or disparity of the text with itself, in its ambiguities, elisions and doublings lies the interpreter's quarry, that which is at once revealed and concealed.

In the bulk of traditional literary criticism, as in culture itself, it being "the much-abused privilege of conscious activity, wherever it plays a part," as Freud remarked, "to conceal every other activity from our eyes" (1900, 774), the unconscious, the repressed, the primary processes, have been severely ignored. Yet, if we are not to privilege conscious activity we should surely not commit the opposite folly. That art is no more than a projection of an artist's conflicts (however "softened" or disguised), that analytical interpretation of literature must be locked within the exclusive domain of the repressed, is an idea which the thinking of Ehrenzweig, Ricoeur, Rogers, Skura and many others seemed fruitfully to transcend. Even regarding the productions of a patient during psychoanalysis, Kris could claim that "so elaborate a configuration, a structure built out of so wide a choice of elements cannot be merely the result of the tendency of the repressed to reach consciousness . . . the integrative functions of the ego are also surely at work" (1956, 446). The comment must apply *a fortiori* to the productions of literary artists.

Criticism which leans upon psychoanalytical discoveries finds itself, therefore, in a quandary. It is unable to determine with any confidence whether it is dealing with a function of the conscious or the unconscious; it is even in doubt as to the nature of its object, or of its "subject." The tendency of those two Cartesian terms, as also of other once clear and distinct polarities – absence and presence, origin and consequence, inside and outside, the spoken and the unspoken – to collapse into each other is no more than symptomatic of the disjunctive (perhaps paternalistic?) logic our rationalist tradition inherits. On the other hand the discovery of the unconscious Other pervasive, indeed inherent, in all discourse, and ultimately levelling of all hierarchies, is a consequence of the deconstructive turn in literary culture. It is at this point that the work of Jaques Lacan, and the heuristic fiction of the textual unconscious becomes of the greatest usefulness.

For whose unconscious do we interpret when we interpret a text?: a character's?; an author's?; a reader's? What cues or clues, landmarks or signposts are available to us, moreover, in a quest for what is, by definition, inherently unknowable? "The main question," says Lacan, "is who speaks? And it is not a question without pertinence."[14]

The radicalness of Freud's theory and of Lacan's return to Freud's theory, Shoshana Felman explains, "was not the discovery of the unconscious – poets had intuited it before him – but the fact that the unconscious *speaks*: that the unconscious has a logic or a signifying structure, that it is structured like a language" (1980, 48), in interlinked chains of displaced signifiers anchored in the key signifiers of Freudian theory: the Father, the Phallus, Death, the Mother.[15] This discovery, that the unconscious speaks, Freud made by *listening* to his hysterical patients, and becoming conscious of his own "reading" of what they were saying, from within himself. What self? His own unconscious was reaching consciousness through a detour through the unconscious of the other. This "inmixture of the subjects" (1972, 45), in Lacan's view, is Freud's great Copernican discovery. At first psychoanalysis posited. an unconscious (inner, private) center of activity as opposed to another (outer, public) center, the conscious, just as the Copernican revolution posited a sun center as opposed to an earth center. What Lacan, returning to it, draws out of the new doctrine is that the unconscious speaks as something other from within the speech of consciousness, which it undercuts or subverts. Thus a cleavage is constituted within consciousness itself, that is, within language, which, rather than being situated between separated realms: a chaotic, preverbal and entirely private turbulence "inside" an individual, and a structured, regularized, rational order "outside" the individual verbally denoted and instituted, is always already other to itself, nonidentical with its meanings. Lacan amusingly illustrates the axiom that "speech communicates what it does not actually say" (1977, 82) and that "the function of language is not to inform but to evoke" (86) by means of a Hindu tale:

> A girl [it begins] is waiting for her lover on the bank of a stream when she sees a Brahmin coming along towards her. She runs to him and exclaims in the warmest and most amiable tones: "What a lucky day this is for you! The dog that used to frighten you by its barking will not be along this

river bank again, for it has just been devoured by a lion that is often seen around here". (82)

Lacan's model of the transaction between reader and text then, is transferential, and quadruply reflexive. Put very simply: both reader and writer (or speaker) are involved in a constant interaction of conscious and unconscious. The writer produces the text as the consequence of an interplay between his own conscious and unconscious, the reader reproduces it by absorbing that interplay in his own. This circuit through the Other (one's own or the other's) is what constitutes the intersubjectivity of linguistic communication and is what Lacan means by his gnomic saying: "the unconscious is the discourse of the Other" (1977, 172). Thus Lacan follows Freud as Kepler followed Copernicus when he established the bifocal ellipse rather than the unifocal circle as a model of "celestial revolutions." Lacan's reading of Freud makes discourse itself "elliptical": lacunary like an ellipsis; bifocal like an ellipse. The pun is a brilliant Lacanian *jeu d'esprit*.

Jean Bellamin-Noel[16] has developed the idea of the "textual unconscious" and of a form of psychocriticism he calls textanalysis along these Lacanian lines. The "textual unconscious" is, he frankly admits, a heuristic construct, like Freud's own primal myths. Like other such constructs in the physical as well as the human sciences, it depends for its validification upon being a model for hypotheses which work in practice, that is, enable a more comprehensive coherence than before to be perceived in an anomalous or chaotic field. If we posit such a textual unconscious as the object of textanalysis, of the interpreter's activity, we are enabled to circumvent the double "specular" and speculative traps of author's intention and reader's response. We are enabled to circle around again to a point *above* the old New Critical formalism with its protective "Stop" signs around the supposed "objectivity" of the verbal icon – the Intentional Fallacy and the Affective Fallacy – a point from which the textual unconscious (and for that matter the textual conscious) is not perceived as a property of the text but as a function of a pact, or a secret complicity, between reader and writer. The critic-reader (as Felman elsewhere brilliantly demonstrated (1978)) is "framed" in his reading. If the making of the text was a displacement by the author of unconscious interests, valencies, obsessions onto the formal and fictional components of the text, it is with his own unconscious interests, valencies, obsessions, that the reader responds, to what, however, is "there," has spoken, in the text, to solicit the response. As Green puts it, "The textual unconscious is present in the text's thematic articulations, its brutal silences, its shifts of tone, and especially in the blemishes, incongruities and neglected details which only interest the psychoanalyst" (1978, 285); later he adds a rider to the effect that

> if someone is to be helped here, it is certainly not the author, who could not care less, but the analyst-interpreter, who helps himself through seeking to comprehend the emotions the text awakens within him. Thus the patient, the potential analysand, is not the author as everyone believes and fears, but the analyst himself. (1978, 278)

The reader is analysand to the text, rather than knowing and superior analyst; but he is analyst too, and the text analysand, that which is listened to with the famous free-floating attention – and with inevitable countertransference. It is the imagined transferential relationship that moves us, that is the scene of the action and the locus of interpretation. Neither text nor reader remains neutral, or inert, undergoing no change. The unconscious – the veiled – in both come under scrutiny, though virtually, not actually, since we speak of the domain of the symbolic. By the same token it is not infantile *causes* of a protagonist's jealousy or anger or whatever that are discovered by psychoanalytical criticism, but infantile *structures*. These distillations of fantasy, objects of each other's rage, fear or desire, are proxies for their primal counterparts, the objects of infantile rage, fear or desire. What comes into view is not a specific (alleged) infantile trauma but the undying child in all of us. The process of working through secondary and primary processes – the author's embodied in the text, the reader's

intuited through a convergence of empathy and introspection –
is thus a four-way process, circular (or rather elliptical) and
perpetually renewable as archaic emotions are reiterated and
recycled.

In the theater, immediate to our senses, conflicts of all kinds
are exhibited, played out and worked through. Immediate in
one sense, but certainly not transparent, for upon the stage a
text speaks through its slippery language, its constellation of
impersonated figures which are always already mediated for
us, their guarded or masked, ambiguous or disingenuous
dialogue relayed through the interpretations of actor and
director. Green (and Hamlet) agree that "the text functions like
a mirror held to the reader – seer and seen in the same person"
(Green, 1985, 24). The theater maximalizes reflection, its
dramatis personae holding up a multiplicity of mirrors,
mirroring themselves, each other, parts of themselves, parts of
us.

Who or what, after all, are they, these dramatis personae?
When we ask, "What is it that 'Pericles' *wants*?; or 'Imogen', or
'Posthumus', or 'Leontes', or 'Prospero'?" we ask the central
heuristic question, but about whom do we ask it, and with
what degree of objectivity can we answer it?

The history of Shakespeare criticism is the history of
attempts to ground readings in objective criteria; but the
insistent themes of twentieth century epistemology which
have undermined older certainties about both "subjects" and
"objects" enable us perhaps to step beyond the rationalist
dichotomy.

The protagonists in these dramas provide foci for our
temporal perception, enable us to connect present and past
event, origin and issue. They also provide us with objects for
the transference of our own obsessions, our own fantasies.
They are illusions of whole-cloth, lifelike personalities. About
that we will all no doubt agree, but a caveat is nevertheless in
order regarding the status of these so intimately and familiarly
named figures and about my own positioning of them in the
spectrum that goes from writing about "The Girlhood of
Shakespeare's Heroines" to total denial of any analyzable

psychoanalytic reality in fictive characters.[17]

In 1946 (the lecture was origially given in 1933) L.C. Knights launched his famous polemical attack upon the psychological realism of the older Bradleyan character analysis, and the gross error of endowing figurative constructs with being, self, a quasi-empirical identity or individuality, as if they were or might be familiar friends or acquaintances. It would be an equally gross error, however, to assume that the proper-naming of characters, the use, in exposition, of "as if alive" formulations concerning speech and event and inferred motivation necessarily entailed a naive realism. Not long after the derisively entitled "How many children had Lady Macbeth?" the expanded English version of Ernest Jones's psychoanalytical *Hamlet and Oedipus* appeared in paperback. Ernest Jones fell a victim to the *rhetoric* of psychological realism when, in setting out to interpret the Hamlet story, he writes, for example, "As a child Hamlet had experienced the warmest affection for his mother" (1955, 91) or, "In reality his uncle incorporates the deepest and most buried part of his own personality" (100), thus feeding the flames of the New Critical formalism of Knights and Cleanth Brooks, with their counter-invocation of "dramatic poem," of "precise, particular image" and of "expanded metaphor" as the sole object of literary study. Radicalized, this meant a denial of the feasibility of a represented human being in drama altogether: "The persons, ultimately, are not human at all, but purely symbols of a poetic vision" (Wilson Knight, 1930, 16). Shakespearean criticism faced (and still faces, in newer deconstructive modes) a disjunctive choice: between an interpretative strategy which sets out to discover poetic or philosophical themes articulated in the artful and evocative patterning of the "words on the page" and the connotations of image clusters, or one that sets out to diagnose the problems of a tragic protagonist on the model of a case history. Too little attention was paid at that time to Jones's exposition, in the very same book, of the function of condensation, splitting and doubling in fictional narration. His discussion of the decomposition of realistically conceived "character" into the figments and fragments and projections of psychic need could have served as a useful bridge to a third possibility, namely, in the view proposed in these pages, an interpretative strategy which aims to discover an informing or generating fantasy, or ensemble of fantasies, in each play. Such fantasy manifests itself in verbal figure and texture in a spectrum of expressive deformations; it shapes the whole and the "parts" – those threatening or seductive personifications which mediate and enable the work of transference. To chart the vicissitudes of desire in these textual personages, is, therefore, to enter the Lacanian ellipse; for these stories are related (in both important senses) to us, to their audience: it is our response they trigger. "Is it not," Green therefore asks, "that the theater is the best embodiment of that 'other scene', the unconscious? It is that other scene" (1979, 1). Hence to read it, is also to read ourselves.

But is it not ourselves that we have always read in our reading of literature? The very notions we have of what we ourselves are is in large part derived from literature, especially drama. Our very word for the entities we conceive ourselves to be – persons – is derived from the theater: from the actor's mask or *persona* – that through which the sound comes. As our word for the congeries of traits we suppose ourselves to possess, or the inner strength with which we like to think we are endowed, is derived from the written or engraved mark or sign which is the beginning of literature. In a masterly study which postscripts a collection of papers on *The Identities of Persons* (1976), Amélie Rorty distinguishes between the uses and environments of our lexicon of "person" terms and traces their evolution in response to cultural transformations. She sets out the differences between such notions as "hero," "character," "figure," "person," "self," "individual" in terms of the variables of cultural change – sociological, economic, legal or constitutional, psychological. Characters, she says, are defined and limited; their assemblage of traits can be enumerated: "In the theory of character there is no mind-body problem . . . nor do they have identity crises, since they are not presumed to be strictly unified . . . They appear in novels by Dickens, not those by Kafka"; whereas the concept of person is grounded in the notion of a unified center of choice and action, therefore of liability and responsibility. While characters are "loose conglomerates of powers and gifts, persons are inviolably unitary and answerable to law and judgement." Further distinctions and ramifications arise. "Selves" are defined as being in conscious possession of their properties, especially their most intimate – experiences, memory, identity – which they can lose (becoming thereby 'alienated' or insane). Whereas "individuals" are "unique, indivisible centers of integrity and difference," whose rights as such are inalienable (299–314, passim).

What do we find in plays by Shakespeare? There will be a mix and overlap, as there might be in any historical period or in any rich and heterogeneous art. There are apparitions and presences, gods and ghosts in Shakespeare, besides the above; but generally speaking let us say of major protagonists, the criteria for character interpretation that we find will be those we seek, those that we are capable of finding, those that we are culturally or educationally conditioned to find. I invoke Rorty's clarification of concepts in order to counter the double accusation: of anthropomorphism, and of anachronism which will be brought against any attempt to employ psychoanalytic insights in the reading of characters in Shakespeare's plays. For the point I draw from her skilful analysis is this: just as we view ourselves, construct ourselves and our stories through the various conceptualizations she discusses, so do we view the personae in our fictions through the very same prism. This will be the justification for any nonhistoricist reading of older literature (reading which ignores, for instance, Elizabethan psychological theories as an interpretative tool), for if we do not wish older works to become fossilized, simply archeological, we *must* employ our contemporary conceptions in interpreting them. Both present and past are thus more fully understood. Rorty shows how the conceptions of person have evolved, how the earlier still inform the later, just as in Freud's archeology of the psyche. Rorty stops with "individuals," but she might have continued: with *psyches*, certainly, seen as a constant co-presence and interplay of conscious and unconscious activity, and finally (for the nonce) with *subjects* – linguistic constructs – as contemporary conceptions of human being. It appears then that we do in fact always read literary narrative fictions as we are and as we see ourselves, which is, as they have made us, and made us see ourselves.

My project therefore is to attempt to see these later plays of Shakespeare through our contemporary eyes, to attempt to understand them as other to ourselves and yet profoundly in touch with what we understand of ourselves.

Such an approach must be extremely flexible. It will interpret the manifestly realistic actions and utterances of the realistically represented characters in their represented environment, using discursive secondary process methods of reasoning and the ability to comprehend cause and effect to determine the reason for and significance of behavior. It will also institute a new internal dialogue between portraiture and poetry, requiring us to open ourselves to language in another way; it will invite us to intuit, to resonate, to remember, or for that matter, to forget, it will demand that we be attentive to the polyphony of the text. One has only to listen to poetry, says Lacan, "for a polyphony to be heard, for it to become clear that all discourse is aligned along the several staves of a score" (1977, 154). Whether we think of this polyphony of discourse as vertical chords – slips of the tongue, or text, which reveal layers of fear or fantasy to which we do not normally have access – or as the counterpoint of characters, objects of each other's rage, fear or desire, each inscribing individual and separate melodic trajectories; whether, in other words, we locate textual polyphony in puns or in personae, the apt notion itself serves notice that it is no simple mimesis of imitation – individuals with which we have to do but rather a complex and total orchestration. It is the whole text that speaks, in sound, in syntax, in symbolization, in suggestion and evocation, in a constant interplay between primary and secondary processes. "We have learnt a subtler process of involvement, of implicating psychoanalysis in literature" (Felman, 1980, 146) than the older case history approach could command, and new possibilities of synthesizing literary and psychological knowledge open up. We construe, with what analytical knowledge we can muster, and with what analytic intuition we can recruit, the deformed, absurd, or irrational in our texts, and in so doing we resurrect the obsessive other stories, the archaic other scenes that their repetitions or reiterations or digressions betray. Lacan's homology of language and the unconscious – "the unconscious is structured like a language" (1972, 45; 1977, 172) – has relocated and reconceived the oneiric, salvaged the unconscious from the realm of purely private neurosis. We could as soon today excise the unconscious, in theory and practice, from our lexicon of mind as we could excise the conscious, or as we could find ourselves upon another planet. This domestication should enable us to approach a literary text – Shakespeare's in particular – postpsychoanalytically: not only as a work of patterned art whose linguistic and conceptual amplitude and subtlety is, quite literally, inexhaustible, but also as if it were a series of dreams one wished to interpret, dreams exhibiting the features that dreams exhibit: condensations, displacements, doublings, splittings, pictographs, and the cunning diversionary tactics of the covert will to reveal and to express.

The questions that arise for criticism are manifold: whether, how, and with what degree of methodological confidence this oneiric mode of reading can be established; whether we can solder together rival discourses – textualist, humanist, formalist; whether our understanding of tragicomedy can in this way be advanced. It is in the context of these questions that the following essays occur; they may perhaps contribute towards the finding of solutions, but their value will rest in whatever capacity they may have to reilluminate the dramas to which, of which, and through which they speak.

2

The perils of Pericles

A thing which has not been understood inevitably reappears;
like an unlaid ghost, it cannot be laid to rest until the
mystery is solved and the spell broken.

(Sigmund Freud, "Little Hans")

Pericles, first of Shakespeare's four romance narratives of
vicissitude, loss and restoration, is usually regarded as the
most tentative, fumbling or inchoate of the four, or not
entirely Shakespeare's at all. Critics have been made unhappy
not only by a text probably transcribed in part from memory,
but also by the Gower narrator's laboured tetrameters, the
jerky tempo of frame narration and dramatized episode, the
curiously "phlegmatic" or "passive" character of the protagonist, and the outlandish events. It is only, it is widely felt, in Act
III, with the death of Pericles' wife and the birth of his
daughter, that the true Shakespearean fire breaks forth from
the flint.

It is certainly a very weird play. Severed heads, more storms
and shipwrecks than most readers can confidently count, the
miraculous preservation of persons alive under water or dead
and unburied on land, a denouement which mixes, if not
hornpipes and funerals, at least brothels and betrothals, and a
remarkably accident-prone protagonist. "Most critics," says
Ernest Schanzer,

are agreed that, while Acts III, IV and V are substantially

Shakespeare's, Acts I and II are not. The questions to be asked, therefore, are: Who is the author of Acts I and II? And how did the non-Shakespearean first two acts come to be joined to the Shakespearean last three acts? (1965, xxi)

I would like to ask quite other questions of this text, which seems to me, so far from being fractured, to possess a degree of unity bordering on the obsessive. I shall hope to show that a reading *of*, rather than round, *Pericles'* strangenesses, a reading attentive to the oneiric dimension of its symbolism and the dream-like aspects of its representations, will give the play a rather different specific gravity than is usually attributed to it, and will enable us to find it, once again, convincing. "Till the closing of the theaters in 1642," Ernest Schanzer tells us, "*Pericles* seems to have been one of Shakespeare's greatest stage successes" (xli). I would like to return the presently undervalued *Pericles* to the canon, finding it, precisely because it is closer to primary process, more anomalous, "crude," absurd, strange, a representation of elemental and universal fantasy of great power.

The story of Pericles is impossible, of course. So, André Green reminds us, is the tragedy of Oedipus. "How can the life of a single man pile up such a set of coincidences?" (1979, 18). He continues, "It is not for the psycho-analyst to answer; but rather for the countless spectators of *King Oedipus* who might say, with Aristotle, 'a convincing improbability is preferable to what is unconvincing even though it is possible'." What is "convincing"? Green's answer is implicit in his account of his project: "The aim of a psycho-analytic reading is the search for the emotional springs that make the spectacle an affective matrix in which the spectator sees himself involved and feels himself not only solicited but welcomed, as if the spectacle were intended for him." It is with the identification of this matrix, and with the investigation of the symbolic activity which allows us access to it, that I shall be engaged.

The questions I would ask, then, emerge from the following reflections. It is not in dispute that the father/daughter theme in the play is its dominant concern, repeated time after time and, in the reunion scene, treated with an admirably expressive pathos, not granted, for example, to Rosalind's father, or Hero's, who also have their lost daughters returned to them. Why then is the axis of the play's action skewed? It is after all the story of Pericles, but Pericles does not become a father until Act III. At the peak of his fortunes his hard-won wife is snatched from him, his newly-born daughter left motherless in his charge. Then indeed he rages against the storm in language reminiscent of Lear, man of sorrows, and daughters. But the child is immediately abandoned to the care of foster parents. And what of his role up to that point? Is it really a kind of marking time, or fragments of a cobbled together or corrupt text, or the work of an inferior collaborator? Or rather a chapter in what Coppelia Kahn sees as Shakespeare's lifelong pursuit of "a dramatic and psychological strategy for dealing not only with our common ambivalence toward our families but specifically with the male passage from being a son to being a father"? (1980, 217). This is useful for the situating of Pericles in the life cycle of sons; but when she continues, "He found it [the strategy] through the romance, in one of its typical patterns of action that I shall call 'the providential tempest' . . . this pattern is that of a journey . . . the individual's passage from emotional residence within the family to independence and adulthood" (218), I believe her invocation of the archetypal symbol of the journey blinds her to a false distinction. "Independence and adulthood" is surely not the opposite, but rather the authentication and clarification of "emotional residence within the family." Do we, in other words, ever "reside" elsewhere than within the family? The "providential tempest" in the story of Pericles will, I believe, reward closer examination, as will the role of the son in the triad father, daughter, suitor which appears again and again in the play.

Pericles is tragicomedy *comme il faut* according to Renaissance theory, which demanded both extreme peril and happy solution; and Pericles' saga of preposterous and totally fortuitous misfortunes can be moralized without difficulty into a vision of longsufferingness (Barker, 1963), princely excellence (Schanzer, 1965) and the wondrous ways of a mysterious

Providence. In this, I suggest, traditional criticism is swallowing the bait of secondary revision which camouflages, or is even itself blind to, the insights that it nevertheless makes available. Traditional criticism characteristically judges the responses of characters to the events which happen to them in terms of ethical, theological or didactic value systems, or interprets them methodically by means of allegory. It is therefore flustered by the gaps, awkwardnesses, inconsequentialities, archaisms it encounters in a text. Indeed, unless we can read in "the progressive, educative 'official' plot" the threatening "repetitive process obscurely going on underneath or beyond it" (Brooks, 1980, 511), we will very probably find "no solution to the problems of *Pericles*" (Edwards, 1976, 41), no alternative to the dismissal of *Pericles* as a mere blue print, or rehearsal, for the greater plays to follow.

T.S. Eliot once said that "meanings" in poetry were like the meat the burglar throws to the house-dog to keep him quiet while it gets on with its proper business. He was, perhaps, paraphrasing Freud, who remarked, drily, that "it is the much abused privilege of conscious activity, wherever it plays a part, to conceal every other activity from our eyes" (1900, 774). We need to cap these gnomic sayings with the programmatic Lacan, who, intent on that "other activity," that "proper business," says, "every unsuccessful [verbal] act is a successful, not to say 'well turned', discourse . . . and exactly in the right quarter for its word to be sufficient to the wise." (1977, 58) The passage of interpretation from signifier on the stage – perhaps odd or crude to the rationally disciplined eye – to signified of "that other scene" ("Is it not that the theater is the best embodiment of that 'other scene', the unconscious? It is that other scene," Green, 1979, 1), requires a reading "wise" to the "tentacular network" of the normally forgotten or repressed, for, and I quote Green again, "in the long succession of signifiers in linked sequence which constitutes the work, the unconscious signified rises . . . from the gulf or absence in which it resides . . . not in order to express what has to be said, but in order to indicate, by veiling it, what needs to be hidden" (1979, 28). "Every literary narrative," says Geoffrey Hartman,

"contains another narrative . . . discontinous and lacunary"
(1978, 102). In order for "the outward movement of the plot to
become an inward movement of the mind" (Skura, 1980, 212)
it is this other narrative that we must attempt to pursue.

One cannot do better than to begin at the beginning, for this
is a play which begins with a bang. The presenter, Gower, puts
the audience in complete possession of the ugly facts, and the
quite extraordinary circumstances in which the young preten-
der to the hand of the Syrian princess makes his suit. There is a
riddle to be explicated and the cost of failure to do so is
graphically depicted by a gruesome row of severed heads: the
remains of previous contenders in this risky enterprise. This is
not an inviting scenario. It is, as the audience knows, a classic
double bind: if he solves the riddle he falls a prey to Antiochus'
rage at being discovered. If he doesn't, he dies. Freudian
symbologists will immediately identify a castration fantasy.
Traditional criticism has chosen to ignore or play down any
such specificity in the threat, repressing its terrors and
regarding it simply as a rather melodramatic launching pad for
Pericles' adventures. It is, for example, simply "by the
discovery of hidden evil," according to Traversi, that Pericles is
"driven . . . to abandon his first dream of felicity" (1969, 265).

Traditional criticism, in fact, has not taken the opening
quite seriously. If we do take it, and the fantasy that it
represents, seriously, however, if we decide not to detach so
startling an opening from its unconscious moorings we will at
once discover a great deal else that suddenly figures in Pericles'
responses, much as Napoleon's hat will suddenly emerge from
among the leaves of a tree, in the children's puzzle game used
by Leclaire and Laplanche as a model for the absent presence of
unconscious representations.[1] Note, for example, the timbre,
and the content, of Pericles' opening speech at his first sight of
the beautiful daughter of Antiochus, "apparelled like the
spring" (I.i.12), in whose face, it seems, "sorrow were ever
ras'd, and testy wrath/Could never be her mild companion"
(17–18). Conventional enough, no doubt, on the face of it, these
praises, but not every young lover admires in his mistress the
absence of attributes (sorrow, wrath) not usually associated

with youth and love at all. More is to come. Where Antiochus likens his daughter to the golden apples of the Hesperides, defended by "deathlike dragons" (27, 29), Pericles associates the gratification of his desire with the dangerous and forbidden fruit whose eating is the source and origin in Genesis of sexual guilt, and of death:

> You gods, that made me man, and sway in love,
> That have inflam'd desire in my breast
> To take the fruit of yon celestial tree
> (Or die in th'adventure), give me your helps
> As I am son and servant to your wills (19–22)

What, in this context, can we make of the homiletic meekness with which he turns to Antiochus:

> Antiochus, I thank thee, who hath taught
> My frail mortality to know itself,
> And by those fearful objects to prepare
> This body, like to them, to what I must;
> For death remembered should be like a mirror,
> Who tells us life's but breath, to trust it error.
> I'll make my will then, and as sick men do,
> Who know the world, see heaven, but feeling woe,
> Gripe not at earthly joys as erst they did (41–55)

Is this not, Christian-stoical though it may seem, somewhat cold for an ardent lover? Is there not the trace of more than a conventional *contemptus mundi* here? A dyspepsia, a melancholy, a lassitude of the will to live and love? This young lover, it seems, is preternaturally ready to envisage his own body in the image of an (already) severed head, preternaturally ready to "make his will . . . as sick men do." He bequeaths, he says, his "riches to the earth from whence they came;/But [his] unspotted fire of love" to the Princess (52–3). The odd splitting and the opposition draw attention to an unspoken tension within the rhetoric. The riches that he bequeaths to Mother Earth can only in the context be his body – rich to him as to any man – and it is this body that stands in opposition to the "unspotted" fire of love. It, therefore, by implication, is what is spotted. The sense of carnal taint is the stronger for the evasive displacement. This suggestion of a sexual anxiety in Pericles' deference to the father of his hoped for bride, magnetizes the apparantly banal figures of speech in Antiochus' warning: "because thine *eye*/Presumes to reach, all the whole *heap* must die .../Yon ... princes/Tell thee, with speechless *tongues* .../And with dead *cheeks* advise thee to desist" (32–9 passim; my italics). The body imagery speaks a subtle and menacing sexuality, at once desire and threat.

It is upon this textual ground, so to speak, that the seed of the riddle falls. We, of course, know the answer to the riddle because we have been told of the incest; and for that reason we may miss its central symbolic import, its own crucial condensation. Let us recall it:

> I am no viper, yet I feed
> On mother's flesh which did me breed.
> I sought a husband, in which labor
> I found that kindness in a father.
> He's father, son, and husband mild;
> I mother, wife – and yet his child. (64–9)

The riddle, it will be noticed, is a riddle because it introduces a third, complicating term into the incest relation between father and daughter: the absent mother. Antiochus is father and husband to his daughter quite literally. How is he her son, she his mother? The expression "feeding (like a viper) upon mother's flesh" is metaphorically tenable for the daughter whether taken to mean simply "taking that which belongs to my mother," or whether relayed through the prior metaphor which makes man and wife one flesh (cf. *Hamlet*, IV.iii.52). Shakespeare's innovation was to make the implied speaker the daughter rather than Antioch as in older versions of the tale.[2] There is a moment during which the solution of the riddle hovers indeterminately between father and daughter: the viper might pick up the previous Eden associations and so keep the riddle's "I" within the feminine orbit, or it might be phallic and so masculinize the whole grotesque image. That Pericles himself is the reader of the riddle, hence our conduit to it, is important in this respect, especially in the theater. There is a certain double-take, therefore, in the deciphering of the riddle. The daughter feeds upon her mother's rightful possession – her own father; but Antiochus too can be said to feed upon mother's flesh – the issue of the mother who is (or was) his own wife. Antiochus is father and husband to his daughter literally but it is only by trope that he is her son, she his mother. It is just this metaphorical condensation that the riddle performs, making Antiochus' daughter/wife his surrogate mother: "he's father, *son*, and husband mild" (my italics).

The riddle is constructed like a dream as Freud expounded the dream-work. It is the dream work methodized: condensation, displacement, representation in pictorial image all cunningly tricked out by secondary revision into the form of the conventional riddle. The absurdities, or catachreses, are instantly penetrated by Pericles, as if the enigma were to him transparent. As indeed it is. "All love the womb that their first being bred" (I.i.107), he says, summing up the meaning of the King's evil; but how is this the meaning? Philip Edwards says, "This puts the incest the wrong way round, son and mother" (1976, 145) and suggests textual corruption. Is it not possible that "the wrong way round" is the right way up, the essence of the matter, a parapraxis if you will, or slip of the text – the desire of the mother being shared, in unconscious complicity, by these two mirror-image Oedipal contenders?

The traumatic experience at Antioch precipitates Pericles' return home, causes his subsequent flight, hence his first shipwreck, hence his arrival in Pentapolis and so forth; but its function as causal event in a linear series does not exhaust its significance. Indeed, we can read the play's events as causing the Pericles story, but we can also read the Pericles story as motivating the events. Drama is peculiarly the art of the present tense, but in its present, as in all presences, is contained the unrecognized past, the other "uncensored draft" of the history (Lacan, 1977, 51). As psychoanalysis teaches us, "What is forgotten is recalled in acts." Lost to conscious memory the past reproduces itself as an unmastered force in the present. We "follow" the fable unfolding before us "with cunning delays and ever-mounting excitement" (Freud, 1900, 363), as a tissue of surprises, as if their end were undetermined; at the very same time we move backwards through a retrospective succession of partial recognition scenes. We move back and forth in a shuttle which enables us to find relationships between the end towards which we progress and the beginning to which we return ("to know the place for the first time?"). Drama, the supremely metaleptic art, resembles, as Freud observed, the "remembering, repeating and working through" of psychoanalysis more than any other form of narrative.[3]

Interestingly, in *Pericles*, because of the narrator Gower, the dual textual functions of relating and enacting are separated. Gower is the only continuous narrator/presenter in Shakespeare. Like the chorus in *Henry V* or Time in *The Winter's Tale*, but unlike other mediating or parabastic figures he *only* addresses the audience, never the dramatis personae.[4] This has the effect of distancing or framing the events, and creating a split in the audience between empathetic participation and critical awareness somewhat as in the Brechtian alienation effect. Only here, since Gower is a character accompanying the whole play, and since the historical Gower has already told the story before in the *Confessio Amantis*, the effect is of a *mise-en-abyme*, a telling within a telling. What is shown and what is told seems fairly arbitrary. Events (some of which we have ourselves witnessed) are recapitulated, other events are anticipated in narrative discourse; a nodal change-producing occurrence is mimed, futher events, unrepresentable practically speaking, like the storms and shipwrecks, are reported. Gower's punctuation of the sequence of direct dramatic enactment by alternating narration and dumb-show foregrounds the question of selection and deletion in narration itself; for that matter the question of the authentic as against the authenticated – the re-told. The Gower figure offers his tale to the audience "for restoratives"; he steps out on stage between the audience and the dramatis personae; he interferes. He constantly requests his audience to conjure up for themselves events anticipated or recapitulated: "In your imagination hold/This stage the ship" (III.Chorus. 58–9). I suggest that we can regard him as a kind of threshold figure – indeterminately analyst and censor, a mediator both vehicle and obstacle. It is as if either the unconscious of the text, like an analysand, strove to communicate a deeper, more inward substance, but was constrained by some inner resistance to offer a processed or pre-packaged version. Or, as in Peter Brooks' notion of "the erotics of form,"[5] as if the text was leading us on with pre-images to some anticipated consummation or resolution yet delaying progress by returns and repetitions. We are sensitized by Gower's mediation to levels of consciousness, and to functions of the telling. Gower remembers, and recounts the story, Pericles reenacts it, and the reenacting itself, *en abyme*, is a compulsive repetition.

What Antiochus thus triggers in Pericles, by way of the condensations of primary process fantasy, is, we intuit, a repetition of himself, an unconscious recognition. Antiochus is his uncanny double; and the progress of the play is the haunting of Pericles by the Antiochus in himself, the incest fear which he must repress and from which he must flee. For Pericles, who, it will be recalled, referred to himself as "son" to Antiochus (I.iv.24, 27), already at the outset, is, as we have seen, in the grip of the oedipal guilt which Freud, in "The Ego and the Id" characterizes as "the pure culture of the death instinct . . . [which] often enough succeeds in driving the ego into death, if the latter does not fend off its tyrant in time by the change round into mania" (1923, 394). Pericles is indeed very nearly driven into death or mania as the play proceeds, but we are not, I submit, to see this as a matter of contingent circumstance alone. Rather, to understand *Pericles* is to see that the Pericles figure – the Periclean fantasy – is always already death-driven.

Let us once more attend to the drama's text as it proceeds with its articulation of the fantasy it both veils and reveals.

The predicament presented in Act I, Scene i, produces a delayed action, like a time bomb. Pericles abandons his courtship, of course, flees Antioch, and goes back home to Tyre; but there he falls into an inexplicable melancholy. He is surrounded by courtly pleasures; his thoughts have "revolted" against the "sweetest flower," once, but no longer, desired; danger is at a distance, in Antioch, and yet he can find no peace.

> Why should this change of thoughts,
> The sad companion, dull-ey'd melancholy,
> [Be my] so us'd a guest as not an hour
> In the day's glorious walk or peaceful night,
> The tomb where grief should sleep, can breed me quiet?
> (I.ii.1–5)

Why, indeed? On the face of it he does have a plausible reason for fear, and for the flight he decides upon. The long arm of the King, whose secret he discovered, will surely pursue him and

> With hostile forces he'll o'erspread the land,
> And with [th'ostent] of war will look so huge,
> Amazement shall drive courage from the state,
> Our men be vanquish'd 'ere they do resist,
> And subjects punish'd that ne'er thought offense. (I.ii.24–8)

The apparent plausibility of this argument must strike us as disingenuous. Its worst-case reasoning is exaggerated, unnerved. It is surely odd for a prince so avidly to envisage defeat, and critics have been properly dismayed at such strangely unrulerlike behavior. How can we account for it? The speech continues thus:

> Which care of them, not pity of myself –
> Who [am] no more but as the tops of trees
> Which fence the roots they grow by and defend them –
> Makes both my body pine and soul to languish,
> And punish that before that he would punish. (29–33)

The disavowal of self-pity suggests its presence, and we note the insistence on the notion of punishment (as opposed for example to revenge or retaliation). Why so much punishment? What crime has been committed (by Pericles) that his thoughts should be so full of punishment? What, moreover, in this deviant syntax, is the subject of the first "punish" in line 33? It is, or it should be, "care of them," which precedes the embedded subordinate clause. "Care of them," however, requires a third person verb. The absence of such a form derails the syntax at that point and generates a search for a possible alternative. If we read "punish" as an infinitive (correlative to "to languish") our alternative subject becomes "soul." Thus: "Care of them makes my body pine, and my soul to languish and to punish that (myself) before he (Antioch) does." Pericles needs the remonstrances of his loyal and candid counsellor (51–124) to crystallize the decision to set sail from Tyre, and to justify the decision as the action of a noble Prince ready to remove himself, a *casus belli*, from the scene; but the packed syntax reveals to us that it is a self-inflicted punitive suffering from which he flees. Why? A powerful potential enemy is an ostensible reason for his flight. That that potential enemy is an intimidating father-figure, law-maker, and beheader, possessed of a (significantly nameless) daughter/mother/bride – "an O without a figure"? (cf. *Lear* I.iv.193) – is suggestive of preliminary conditions; but the immediate precipitating source of his dread – an archaic energy at work like Hamlet's old mole – is specific: it is that *he has uncovered* the King's terrible secret. The primal scene of the play – Act I, scene i – triggers a primal scene fantasy for Pericles, which powers thenceforth his guilt-stricken, haunted, drivenness.[6]

But his sallying forth is not only fugue. At all events, as it turns out, it acquires major value and virtue through the role of feeder and saviour he is enabled to play in famine-stricken Tarsus. There, Cleon reports, once fastidious palates now beg for bread, man and wife draw lots to decide who shall die first, there is scarcely strength left to bury the dead, and

> Those mothers who, to nuzzle up their babes,
> Thought nought too curious, are ready now
> To eat those little darlings whom they loved. (I.iv.42–4)

These are dismaying, and resonant, images to appear in the description of the plight of Tarsus.[7] And he is not permitted to remain a saviour for long. These devouring mothers mark the oscillation of longing and fear, fight and flight which is the rhythm of Pericles' wayfaring. The next phase of the action is introduced by Gower again recounting the initiating incest story, and by his dumb show, in which bad news is delivered of pursuit from Tyre. Act II opens with Pericles' address to the elements when he finds himself cast up upon the shore at Pentapolis after the wreck of his escape ship.

Bred on the thunderous eloquence of Lear we may find these lines at first somewhat threadbare; but it is a speech worthy of remark in several respects.

> Yet cease your ire, you angry stars of heaven!
> Wind, rain, and thunder, remember earthly man
> Is but a substance that must yield to you;
> And I (as fits my nature) do obey you.
> Alas, the seas hath cast me on the rocks,
> Wash'd me from shore to shore, and left [me] breath
> Nothing to think on but ensuing death.
> Let it suffice the greatness of your powers
> To have bereft a prince of all his fortunes;
> And having thrown him from your wat'ry grave,
> Here to have death in peace is all he'll crave. (II.i.1–11)

Pericles has every cause for distress at this point – "All perishen of man, of pelf,/Ne aught escapend but himself" (II.Chorus.35–6), but it will be noticed that there is no reference in his lament to the loss of the ship, or the sailors, nor any reference to the trauma of the wreck itself; nor for that matter is there any rejoicing or thanksgiving, however qualified, regarding his own escape. It is a total submission, a capitulation, that he expresses, and the powers to whom he capitulates are given, by the nature and the configuration of the imagery, a distinctly familial cast; the paternal, wrathfully punitive sky elements which it is "his nature" to obey; the maternal ocean from which he has emerged. We note the casting upon rocks, immediately displaced by the rocking motion ("wash'd me from shore to shore") suggesting a cradle, or womb; but he is a castaway upon this rocky shore, breathless and bereft, and it is a "wat'ry grave" from which he has been thrown. The passage is indissolubly ambivalent: whether he wishes or fears this womb/grave is impossible to determine – the condensation is, precisely, a compromise formation. The parent-child configuration gives a particular tinge to the melancholy he expresses, the deep depression, the dispirited craving for death. We discern the backward drift of an unresolved, unnamed preoccupation. We perceive the stance of a son whose rebellious rage against a parental couple – sky-father and sea-mother – has turned inward against himself.

This is the first of the play's sea journeys, which mark the pendulum swing of desire and dread, outgoing and withdrawal in the psychodrama which we follow. The play enacts its complex fantasy by repeated emergings from the sea, repeatedly foiled by the sea tempests themselves – a collusion of both parental figures in a rejecting fury. Pericles is dogged by mischance, but do not these chances "reflect the destiny which has decreed that through flight one is delivered over to the very thing that one is fleeing from" (Freud, 1956, 63)? That the sea, Pericles' constant refuge, and betrayer, giver and taker, destroyer and restorer, is a powerful presence in the play, has escaped no interpreter but its import has been found bewildering. "The unlikelihood of the events," says Philip Edwards,

> the lack of cause-and-effect in the plot, make the play a presentation of images which, while individually they expand into wide and general meanings, yet as a whole sequence withdraw from asserting how things run in this world. We are offered ideas or propositions about love and suffering and chastity, and the relation of them to a divine will, but we are not offered a clue to any meaning lying in the progression of events. The sea, therefore, remains a mystery." (1976, 31)

Yet his own description of "the sea of life, the flow of unaccountable circumstances in which we drift" contains more of the clue he seeks than, it seems, he realizes: "The sea threatens and comforts, destroys and rebuilds, separates and unites" (17). Archetypal symbol of vicissitude in human life –

yes; but "oceanic," it will be recalled, was Freud's term for those fantasies of merging, union and dissolution which are rooted in yearnings for the primal symbiosis of infant and mother; and it is not without relevance to remember the interesting image used by the melancholy wandering Antipholus in *The Comedy of Errors*.[8]

> He that commends me to mine own content
> Commends me to the thing I cannot get.
> I to the world am like a drop of water
> That in the ocean seeks another drop,
> Who, falling there to find his fellow forth,
> (Unseen, inquisitive), confounds himself.
> So I, to find a mother and a brother,
> In quest of them (unhappy), lose myself. (I.ii.33–40)

The mere identification of a symbol is no more than is available in any dictionary of symbols. Simply to name is to vivisect, as Freud himself warned (though he often sinned himself in this respect (see *The Interpretation of Dreams*, 1900, 496–529), failing to distinguish between hallucinatory infantile visual symbolization and subtly complex verbal derivatives). The sea has been with us, and in our iconologies, for a very long time, but there is a pre-Freudian and a post-Freudian way of attending to symbols. In 1899, in his Notes to *The Wind among the Reeds*, Yeats speaks of "some neo-platonist [who] describes the sea as a symbol of the drifting indefinite bitterness of life"; in 1932, in his Notes to *Fighting the Waves*, "A German psychoanalyst," he says, "has traced the 'mother-complex' back to our mother the sea – to the loneliness of the first crab or crayfish that climbed ashore and turned lizard."[9] Yeats makes my point. What the play *Pericles* wonderfully captures, obsessively reiterates, is, indeed, the rhythm of vicissitude in human life, the rhythm of maturation: separation, dispossession, return, under the cross of guilt, where three roads meet. The original loss or lack, or absence, psychoanalytic theory tells us, is always the same; but its individual manifestations are always different, for it is through an endlessly varied chain of displaced signifiers that we strive, in language, to reconstitute the ever-receding, forever lost state of undifferentiated wholeness that was the bliss, and the fate, of the speechless infant.

Yeats' note treats evolutionary biology with considerable poetic license, but let us, adopting his metaphor, pursue the adventures of our "lizard." It is the sequence of his recovery at this point which is particularly worth remarking.

Pericles climbs ashore at Pentapolis, and meets fishermen who have acerbic and foolish-wise things to say about the inequalities of the worldly world, where "the great ones eat up the little ones" (II.i.28) like whales, who would swallow all, "parish, church, steeple, bells and all" (34). The Third Fisherman caps this parable with his own: "when I had been in his belly, I would have kept such a jangling of the bells that he should never have left till he cast bells, steeple, church, and parish up again," (40–3). What the "whale" or sea, casts up is in fact the dripping Pericles: "What a drunken knave was the sea to cast thee in our way!" (58)

Ancient paradigms have suggested themselves as models for the wanderings and sufferings of Pericles, in particular Ulysses, and the long-suffering Job; but in the light of the imagery in which the fishermens' observations are cast, Jonah would seem to be no less suitable a candidate.[10] Not that these figures need be mutually exclusive. Texts wander about the world in each other's company, as we know, no less than romance protagonists. But, it will be remembered, Jonah too fled from commitment, sank deeper and deeper into withdrawal during his three days aboard – a fugue which culminated in the belly of the whale – and was spewed forth to take up his mission again willy-nilly. Once again it is such derivatives of the primal oral infantile fantasies of eating and being eaten which lend support to the theory of "the other story," the repressed, or censored draft. Pericles' first response to the fisherman's questions is that of a passive victim – mere tennis ball (like Bosola) to the waters and the wind, he envisages death and begs only for burial when the cold which "throngs up his veins" (73–5, 77) finally overcomes him; but when the good King Simonides is referred to, and the joust that he plans, at which suitors will "tourney for the love of his fair daughter," Pericles regains a will to live. "Were my fortunes equal to my desires,' he says, "I could wish to make one there" (111–12). Whereupon, hey presto, what should emerge from the sea in the fisherman's net but – his dead father's armour! This is a blessing, obviously, since it provides Pericles with the means to pursue honour, and a bride, at the court of Pentapolis; but for this purpose any treasure chest, or for that matter any suit of armour from the sunken ship would have served. Pericles' father's armour is talisman and symbol as well as blessing. Bequeathed in the father's will, it defended the father as the latter hopes it may defend his son. In the dream language of condensation, wearing it, blessedly belched forth out of the sea, Pericles both is and is safe from, his dead father. He "becomes" his father, legit-imately, even obligatorily, as he sets forth upon his second courtship adventure.

In *Pericles* the psychomachia – the motivations at war within the protagonist, the bonds and bindings, the desires and fears which constitute for him his impossible choice – is not explicit, not immediately to be perceived. We are listening with the third ear, catching the unspoken filtering into discourse in the underhand ways the unspoken has of speak-ing. Ostensibly what Pericles contends with is the weather, the ocean, the winds and the waves; or competing knights at a tourney, but consider the scene of the tourney, or rather the scene which, significantly, takes the place, and at some length, of any staged combat.

The actual tourney, which takes place off stage, is prefaced by a procession of the contender knights each bearing a shield with an emblematic device, and an explanatory Latin tag. On the face of it, and at the level of the represented world of the fable, what we are presented with here is simply a piece of chivalric decoration. We may entertain ourselves (as do the courtiers – the hermeneutic game of emblems was very popular in the seventeenth century) checking the match of tag to enigma, wondering what riddle will come next and what Pericles' contribution will be. The emblem game consisted of pictorializing epigrams or sententiae of extreme and uncontextualized generality: "a black Ethiop reaching at the sun . . . *Lux tua vita mihi*" (II.ii.20–1); "a hand environed with clouds,/ Holding out gold that's by the touchstone tried . . . *Sic spectanda fides*" (36–8); and so on. The connection between image and idea was often enough conventional, but the game became popular and interesting, worth playing indeed, in so far as the images were derived from the motto by rebuslike or arcane associations of one kind or another, or by what we would call today "free" association. The resemblance to the techniques of dream, here as in the first riddle, is again striking: condensation, displacement, pictorialization and secondary revision; and we have a context – threatening parental figures, an imagery of bodily injury, menace and engulfment, which, if not repressed by readers, will magnetize the whole semiotic environment.

We can read the knights, minimally identified and all identical in aim, as essentially all one knight – projections of Pericles himself. We can read these images as mirrors in which Pericles reads himself, or as signifiers given meaning in Pericles' dream. The anomalies, paradoxes or absurdities at the level of the signifier solicit *our* interpretation, the ulterior signifieds, his. The devices are all configurations of ambivalence, the repressed unconscious fear concealed by the decorous mask of the mottos' secondary elaboration which expresses the conventional devotions and tribulations of courtly desire. Thus, while "*Lux tua vita mihi*" suggests an appropriate knightly ardour, the Ethiop in the emblem is (also) a black, or blackened, or shadowed Icarus, an overweening son against the sun. The armed knight that is conquered by the lady bears the unexceptionably courtly message: "*Piu per dolcezza che per forza*" (26–7), but could be taken literally, as is the way of dreams – as an actual conquest by a woman – and so articulates ambivalent wishing and fearing. In the symbology of dreams, crowns and wreaths, metamorphoses of that most fertile of all figures, the circle, are genital displacements upwards.[11] The burning torch turned upside down, to show that "beauty hath his power and will,/Which can as well inflame as it can kill" (34–5) has for motto, *Qui me a lit, me*

extinguit: "Who feeds me puts me out" – again a thralldom of
desire and dread – which plugs, with splendid overdetermina-
tion, into oral, filial and sexual anxieties. The image of the
hand holding out gold from amidst clouds to be tested by the
touchstone (36–7) is surely very strange and obscure unless we
can see an (anal)ogy to infantile anxieties about producing and
withholding, while the "country knight's" own phallic device,
a withered branch with a green tip (43), once again marvel-
lously symbolizes an irresolvable ambivalence of hope and
fear.

Pericles, despite his rusty armour, wins the tourney and
Thaisa's heart; and Simonides, good king, not bedazzled by
outward show, recognizes the inner worth of his impeccably
courteous future son-in-law: but is it courtesy, or a humility
bordering upon a surrendering self-abasement? Perhaps the
most revealing moment in these scenes is the melancholy
knight's own aside immediately after his victory at the
tourney. A triumphant winner at this point, what he says is as
follows:

> [Yon] king's to me like to my father's picture,
> Which tells [me] in that glory once he was;
> Had princes sit like stars about his throne
> And he the sun for them to reverence . . .
> Where now his [son's] like a glow-worm in the night,
> The which hath fire in darkness, none in light. (II.iii.37–44)

At the point of winning his fair bride Pericles' self-
estimation has, strangely, never been lower, nor his guilty
self-abasement more explicit. If we reverse the son/sun
homonym, moreover, the tempting/frightening possibility of
usurping the father figure comes again into view: "And he the
son for them to reverence . . ./Where now his sun's like a
glow-worm in the night." Danger – of supplanting the father –
is inherent in success. That which is dangerous – *pericoloso* –
is embedded in Pericles' name.[12] Moreover the play reiterates
its obsessions in other figures besides Pericles. Simonides,
despite his acceptance of the match, is not immune to paternal
jealousy.

> By Jove, I wonder, that is king of thoughts,
> These cates resist me, he but thought upon. (28–9)[13]

This pang of resentment is at once dissimulated as a testing of his daughter's feelings for "but a country gentleman" who has "done no more than other knights have done" (33). Scene iii concludes with the utmost amity on his part towards Pericles, yet scene v repeats the whole premarital testing sequence, with Simonides acting out a Brabantio-like rage towards Pericles:

> Thou hast bewitch'd my daughter and thou art
> A villain.   (II.v.49–50)

and a blocking father's tyranny to his daughter:

> I'll tame you; I'll bring you in subjection.
> Will you, not having my consent,
> Bestow your love and your affections
> Upon a stranger?   (75–8)

Whether we read Simonides' dissembling as simply for the purpose of testing Pericles' character, or as an acting out of his own fatherly ambivalence ("Nay, how absolute she's in't,/Not minding whether I dislike or no!" (19–20)) is immaterial. The question is how this unwilling son will respond to Simonides' assault. Pericles' initial response is to abase himself, to disavow all aims or claims to Thaisa's hand, to plead like a scolded child. Yet suddenly, at the charge of treachery, he rises to defend his honour at sword's point.

Pericles, it would seem, is a kaleidoscopically wavering character. He oscillates between listlessness and energy, withdrawal and outgoingness, defence or flight and attack. He seeks a wife, a family. He is a responsible king. He can rouse himself to courageous action despite his diffidence, as we have seen, and phonemic ambiguities (son/sun) may serve as cover for a considerable urge to self-assertion. Yet he withdraws, gives up, wanders away, evades, or is foiled. What happens to him is invariably what he fears, not what he hopes, as if the elements conspire with a self-fulfilling prophecy. The chorus which opens Act III images sexual fulfillment, achievement, but at once comes terrible reversal. Pericles loses his wife in a tempest at sea as his daughter is born. In terms of tragic structure this is as it should be: a fall from a height of power and prosperity. But the constant repeat or reiteration of such events is itself a message which solicits our attention. These vicissitudes of fortune can be read, at one level, simply as such. Ostensibly they represent the turn of Fortune's wheel, now up, now down, testing Pericles' powers of endurance with its mutations; but if, at a level more covert, the sea is a displaced signifier of the maternal oceanic, then Pericles' tale is very easily retold. "If what Freud discovered and rediscovers with a perpetually increasing sense of shock has a meaning," says Lacan,

> it is that the displacement of the signifier determines the subjects in their acts, in their destiny, in their refusals, in their blindnesses, in their end and in their fate, their innate gifts and social acquisitions notwithstanding, without regard for character or sex, and that, willingly or not, everything that might be considered the stuff of psychology, kit and caboodle, will follow the path of the signifier. (1972, 60)

Pericles travels out and away and back. He cannot escape, cannot cut the umbilical cord, and cannot resolve the later Oedipal guilt. The sea is indeed his beloved enemy, as the sun-father is his envied and hostile rival. Antiochus represents at the outset, the threatening father figure, and whatever person Pericles seeks is a symbolic personage representing the mother, lost and forbidden. It is therefore always by the incest fear that he is haunted. Derivatives of these primal constellations erupt in language and situation throughout: the very name he gives his daughter is the name of the sea.

It is as such a haunting fantasy, I think, that we can read the report of Helicanus in Tyre of the exposure of Antiochus' incest with his daughter (it is the third time we have been told of it), and of their terrible fate. This report is apparently arbitrarily intercalated between the two scenes in which

Simonides plays the role of a threatening father, rather as in a film when shots from another time and place are interpolated into a sequence to represent an image in the mind. Seated in a chariot with his daughter:

> a fire from heaven came and shrivell'd up
> Those bodies, even to loathing; for they so stunk,
> That all those eyes ador'd them ere their fall
> Scorn now their hand should give them burial. (II.iv.8–12)

The blocking father and the incestuous daughter are dead, indeed, but their nightmare image continues to haunt; the shrivelled bodies stink to high heaven, unburied, preserved mysteriously *as* images of fear and horror and loathing as yet unexorcized.

The nightmare is the obverse of the oceanic dream; the prohibition of its siren lure. It is the tempests at sea, with their lightning and thunder, that repeatedly overthrow him. It is perhaps not without significance that Pericles' address to the storm recalls that of Lear, who would have set his rest upon Cordelia's "kind nursery."

>   O, still
> Thy deaf'ning, dreadful thunders; gently quench
> Thy nimble sulphurous flashes! . . .
> [Thou] storm, venomously
> Wilt thou spet all thyself?   (III.i.4–7)

The jealous, tempestuous sea takes Thaisa, yet once again the sea spews its victims (Pericles himself, or his wife, or his daughter) forth, in the struggle to be born again. The mortal combat between Thanatos and Eros is given in the second part of the play with a verbal felicity and resonance to which no critic can fail to respond. Consider the peculiarly evocative speech in which he consigns Thaisa to the waves, which contains within its compassion ("A terrible childbed hast thou had, my dear;/No light, no fire" (56–7)), the Jonah death-wish, the great desire to be, at last, at peace, beneath the "humming water" and "the belching whale," "lying with simple shells" (62–4).[14]

The recovery of Thaisa in Act III, scene ii is manifestly a compensatory birth or rebirth fantasy: out of the chest/coffin emerges a sweet-smelling "corse." Why does the play need a birth fantasy, and a nourishing father (in Cerimon – "hundreds call themselves/Your creatures" (III.ii.44–5)) when it has the real birth of Marina?; and how can we account for his leaving the babe, that "fresh new seafarer" (III.i.41) to be reared by Cleon and Dionyza while he retreats into the monkish garb of a Nazirite? The tragic reversal of Act III, culminating in the tempest which kills Thaisa, is transformed by amazing happenstance into a happy reunion, with the sea giving up its "dead" and a reconstituted, benign family configuration replacing the monstrous union of the first Act. However, this comic resolution is due to happenstance only in terms of the "official" or exterior plot. If we read "the repetitive process obscurely going on underneath or beyond it" (Brooks, 1980, 511), expressing itself indirectly through the very means which veil it, much of great interest becomes apparent.

The recovery of Thaisa, belched forth from the sea, is a rebirth fantasy in the text, to which we, the audience, are privy, but in the progress of the fable her loss at sea represents regression in Pericles. As his abandonment of his baby daughter to the care of others also indicates, he is still not enfranchized, not ready to accept fatherhood, still haunted by the spectre of incest. Lear, as the Fool tells him, made his daughters his mother; Pericles cannot permit himself to love his daughter, lest he desire her – and when he dares, it is too late.

Years later, he "again thwart[s] the wayward seas . . . To see his daughter, all his live's delight" (IV.iv.10–12), and to bring her home. He finds her, as he believes, in her grave. That Pericles will suffer grievously over this loss hardly needs explanatory comment, but Gower's comment points interestingly to the relation between mourning and melancholia which was in due course (three hundred years and a decade later) to become a Freudian theme. "He swears," Gower informs us, "Never to wash his face, nor cut his hairs; He [puts] on sackcloth, and to sea. He bears/A tempest, which his mortal vessel tears,/And yet he rides it out" (27–31). Tempest-tossed, death-possessed, he has become fixed in the mortified posture which acts out the wish to die that is born of the conviction that he deserves to die.

The play's remedial and recognitive last two Acts will tell us that what Pericles needs is not the return of his wife or the birth of a child but a rebirth for himself. Not until Pericles' lost and found daughter "beget'st him that did [her] beget" (V.i.195) as he puts it, is the tempest which his mortal vessel tears, at last stilled. But is it?; and how shall we integrate into our reading the grotesqueries of Mytilene?

The "absolute" Marina, it will be recalled, is done away with by her jealous foster mother – a figure who reappears as Imogen's stepmother in *Cymbeline*, and, as the witch Sycorax, lurks in the background of Prospero's island. Her own daughter is put in the shade, so she feels, by Marina's surpassing excellence in the womanly arts and virtues. Cleon protests, but is overborne by his Goneril-like queen. This weak and recessive father cannot save his step-daughter from the assault of the dominant mother, since he is undermined by Dionyza's taunts of cowardice. Is Cleon, proxy father for Pericles, also his masochistic self-image? "In the dream," André Green reminds us, "when the dreamer's representation becomes overloaded, the dreamer splits it into two and sets up another character to represent, separately, one or more of his characteristics or affects" (1979, 2).[15] This will prove a useful principle with which to approach the next phase of the play.

Act IV, which follows the adventures of the fatherless Marina, (orphaned also of her faithful old nurse) is, it will be noticed, quite conspicuously full of surrogate parental or quasi-guardian figures including the brothel "family" – the pandar, his bawd wife and their servant Boult – and Lysimachus himself, who, though his age is never mentioned, seems, as governor of the city, authority figure and Marina's patron, more a father than a lover until their betrothal. It is also conspicuously full of imminent rape. Leonine expects the rescuing pirates to ravish Marina; the brothel "family," for whom Marina's virginity at first presented itself as a commercial asset, are later intent upon disabusing themselves of her "peevish" intractability ("We must either get her ravished or be rid of her ... she would make a puritan of the devil" (IV.vi.5–9)); the two gentleman customers are put by her "quirks, her reasons, her master-reasons, her prayers, her knees" (8) "out of the road of rutting forever" (IV.v.9) and the disguised governor Lysimachus is – what? unmanned? derailed? converted? (we shall return to Lysimachus presently) by what the Bawd calls Marina's "virginal fencing" (IV.vi.57).

The classic recourse, in psychoanalytic theory, of the maternally fixated libido is a debased sexual object – prostitute or courtesan. The transformation of Marina into such a figure liberates sexual fantasy, the brothel scenes providing a screen through which the deeply repressed sensuality of Pericles can find release. Thus the remedial fourth-act exorcism-through-exacerbation which characterizes Shakespearean comedy can be seen to be effected through the brothel scenes.[16] Pericles, himself absent from the stage, a monk in his mourning and his melancholy, is replaced by these fantasized figures, whose bawdy eroticism can be allowed free play within the constraining limits, or off-limits, of Marina's charismatic chastity. What strikes us in the sexual metaphors here is that they are sadistic, rather than comic. The overriding theme is not reciprocal sexual play, cheerfully spilling over into verbal play as in the early comedies, or in Mercutio's jesting, nor even the wry consequences of sexual play in the form of venereal-disease punishment which is also usual in Shakespeare. The overriding theme is simply defloration, and the metaphors are fantasies of injury, force, mutilation or cannibalism too threatening to amuse. They at once titillate and alienate by appeals to a voyeurism or sadomasochism not veiled but provoked by the euphemism or metaphor: "Marry, whip the gosling, I think I shall have something to do with you. Come, you're a young foolish sapling, and must be bow'd as I would have you" (IV.ii.86–8); "if I have bargain'd for the joint – Thou mayst cut a morsel off the spit" (130–1); "For flesh and blood, sir, white and red, you shall see a rose (IV.vi.34–6); "Boult, take her away, use her at thy pleasure. Crack the glass of her virginity, and make the rest malleable ... And if she were a thornier piece of ground than she is, she shall be ploughed" (141–5).

The brothel sequence fulfills its exorcist function despite, or within, the control of secondary revision. The drama's seductive fable ensures that the physical act, through the wit, wisdom and self-possession of Marina, the protective bounty of Lysimachus and the good offices of Boult, does not in fact come about. The whole brothel sequence takes something of the form of a protracted, though in the end frustrated, initiation ritual: "My lord, she's not pac'd yet, you must take some pains to work her to your manage," says Boult (63–4); she is to be initiated into "our profession" (7). This, because it is parody of a sort, serves as a species of legitimization; even the commercialization of sex does this. One notes that it is this theme which is made to yield the Shakespearean humour of Boult's final grumbling protest at Marina's excoriation of his trade: "What would you have me do? Go to the wars, would you? Where a man may serve seven years for the loss of a leg, and have not money enough in the end to buy him a wooden one?" (171–3); but read at the level of primary process Marina is a depersonalized sex object for the release of deeply repressed and traumatized libido.

It is at this point that we can take up two nagging questions that have troubled the critics. Why, it is asked, does Thaisa, retrieved from a watery grave by Cerimon, become a vestal in Diana's temple instead of setting forth in search of her husband? "The plot of romantic fiction will have it so," says Hallett Smith (Riverside preface, 1481). It is the answer, not the question that, I suggest, is naive. If we read, not the plot of romance narrative, but the plot of "the other scene," we can see that it is necessary for both Marina's parents to be sexually in abeyance, neutralized, while the screen fantasies of the brothel scenes are taking place. The psychic burden is shifted, so to speak, to the shoulders of the surrogate figures. It is upon similar lines that we can address the second nagging question: What was Lysimachus doing in the brothel in the first instance?

The text is poker-faced. We cannot make out whether he is caught out in a visitation the like of which it is his custom to make – he is certainly familiar enough to and with Boult – and subsequently converted by Marina's spirited virtue; or whether he is covertly investigating – what? – the state of morality in the stews of his city? "I came with no ill intent" (IV.vi.109), he says. Then with what intent did he come? This unsolved mystery is more serious than it seems because it puts into question his relation to Marina, making this brothel-betrothal seem a rather hugger-mugger affair, to say the least. This problem too cannot be solved by appeal to comic genre conventions such as marriages all round or sudden conversion and the like because, first, too much emotional interest is invested in protagonist figures for us to be content with mere plot devices to round off a play. In the second place it is never made clear whether Lysimachus was in need of conversion or not. He remains therefore a split character, indeterminately ravisher and protector. This split, or anomaly, is our clue. For if the dream burden has been displaced to other figures in the way Green describes, and we can read Lysimachus as a representation, or extension of Pericles, then the split in Lysimachus is the unconscious split in Pericles. If therefore, the archaic turbulence of ambivalent desire and dread has been played out in the fantasy, and Marina has been saved by a fatherly figure (and/or a brotherly figure if we see Boult as her immediate saviour), when the young girl is brought to the ailing King, in Act V, to warm him back to life there is a double indemnity against the threat of incest. Pericles and Marina are safe and the way is clear for rebirth and restoration.

When the reunion occurs therefore it is truly miraculous – thaumaturgic. The King's grief has brought him to the point of death; now his healing is enacted before us. His initial resistance as he pushes Marina away, her resemblance to Thaisa, the gradual dawning of his recognition, the reluctance to believe lest it not be so, the fear of too great joy:

O Helicanus, strike me, honored sir,
Give me a gash, put me to present pain,

> Lest this great sea of joys rushing upon me
> O'erbear the shores of my mortality,
> And drown me with their sweetness. O, come hither,
> Thou that beget'st him that did thee beget. (V.i.190–5)

draw their power not only from finely observed human behaviour, but from our intuition of the entrenchedness of defence and repression that has had to be broken through. We must love, said Freud, in order not to fall ill. The pleasure we feel is the measure of the depth of the need, and the deprivation:

> My dearest wife was like this maid, and such a one
> My daughter might have been . . .
>   another Juno;
> Who starves the ears she feeds and makes them hungry
> The more she gives them speech. (106–14)

We witness the paradigmatic moment of the late romances which, in Barber's felicitous formulation "free family ties from the threat of sexuality," whereas the early comedies had freed sexuality from the ties of family (1969, 59–67). "Thou that beget'st him that did thee beget" is, as Barber notes, the secular equivalent of Dante's theogony: "Virgine madre, figlia in tua figlio," and is "the rarest dream that e'er dull'd sleep/Did mock sad fools withal" (V.i.161–2).

Here, clearly, the play cannot remain. For a totality of psychic value in one beloved figure – mother and daughter at once – reproduces the spectre of Antioch. The play offers us a solution to this impasse in the recovery of Thaisa, and the betrothal of Marina to Lysimachus. There is even a separate kingdom available for both the generations, since the recent death of Thaisa's father leaves the throne of Pentapolis vacant for the parental couple.

And yet there is an unresolved indeterminacy in the text which makes it possible to read the ending of *Pericles* not as a mandala closure but as a dizzying return to square one. Consider the strange ambiguities of Pericles' final speech to the restored Thaisa:

No more, you gods, your present kindness
Makes my past miseries sport. You shall do well
That on the touching of her lips I may
Melt, and no more be seen. O, come, be buried
A second time within these arms. (V.iii.39–43)

Eros? Thanatos? Can we say? To die upon a kiss was a
common Renaissance metaphor for consummation; but how
shall we read these words? Does the text crumble to its own
deconstruction at the end, with nothing resolved or exorcized,
but all to be done again? I turn once more to André Green. "We
shall often feel a renewed disappointment," he says, "faced by
[the text's] refusal to take us anywhere except to the point of
origin from which it took its own departure" (1979, 23). Is this
the case in *Pericles*? And is it disappointment that we feel?
Or is this refusal simply a sign that the play has put us in touch
with the familiar ghosts – the desires and the terrors – that
habitually haunt our minds?

3

Cymbeline: the rescue of the King

All creatures born of our fantasy, in the last analysis, are
nothing but ourselves.

(Schiller)

There is a "plethora of story-lines," as Barbara Mowatt puts it,
in *Cymbeline*:

> The Snow White tale of a princess, her evil stepmother, a
> home in the woods and a deathlike sleep; a Romeo-and-
> Juliet-like tragedy of a banished lover, an unwanted suitor,
> deaths and near-deaths; a medieval folktale of a chastity-
> wager and an evil Italian villain. (1976, 55)

There are also Roman legions and (real) British chronicle
history. The components of these stories are quite regular
features of romance narrative, but in *Cymbeline* they generate
weirdly replicative configurations: Imogen and Posthumus
both survive two lost brothers, both are orphans, and both have
been brought up in the same household by a step- or foster
parent, as have one set, Imogen's, of lost brothers. We make the
acquaintance of a foster father, a bereaved father, a blocking
father, a substitute father-mother (Belarius), a surrogate father
(Lucius), a father-god, a visionary father-and-mother who
appear to Posthumus in a dream or hallucination, and a
mother-father in the shape of the King who at the end

announces himself, in wonder "A mother to the birth of three" (V.v.369). A poison disguised as a prophylactic becomes a cordial whose effects appear lethal; into (or out of) the play's orbit floats a trunkless head, a headless trunk, and a false trunk from which a man emerges; Imogen is the victim, twice, of a species of (unconsummated) bed-trick, once with a slanderer sent by her husband to test her, and once with the dead body of her rejected suitor whom she takes to be her husband; she is wakened by an aubade (though she has not been in bed with a lover) and laid to rest with an elegy (though she is not dead); Posthumus changes from Roman to British clothing and back a number of times; and there are more recognitions and revelations in Act V than most readers can confidently count. Would one not be justified in regarding repetition of such high frequency as a kind of representational stutter? Or does the play precisely thus speak of what it can only partly say?

Cymbeline presents some of the knottiest problems in Shakespeare genre criticism, appearing to be neither fish, flesh nor good red herring; readable neither as history, comedy nor romance. Though placed after *Pericles* in the accepted chronology of the final plays, it is in many ways more akin to the earlier *All's Well* than to the other three romances. As in *All's Well*, the heroine sets out in pursuit of an errant husband and the hub of the interest lies in the affairs of the young married couple, who are estranged. Yet much is made of the return of Cymbeline's long-lost sons and the family reunions, as in the romances, which bridge the wide gap of time inserted into the dramatic action by the interwoven desires of two generations. As in *All's Well* it is important that a wasteland-sick king is made well. *Cymbeline* is the last of the plays to make a bold young woman, rather than her father, its main protagonist. In that respect Imogen is more akin to the independent daughters of the earlier courtship comedies than to the thaumaturgic daughters of the three last plays; yet she is far from being free of a controlling parent as are Beatrice, Viola, Olivia and Rosalind. She is what one might call a post-tragic heroine, abused, vilified, hunted, and not in possession of crucial knowledge. She may know what she is doing when she defies her tyrant father ("I beseech you, sir,/Harm not yourself with your vexation,/I am senseless of your wrath" (I.i.133–5)), but she (like everyone else in *Cymbeline*, indeed)[1] is at every point unaware of or deceived about the major facts effecting her situation. Where Rosalind and Viola act out their maverick fantasies with a blithe insouciance, adopting their boy's garb as a ploy to be enjoyed, while it lasts, for the mastery it gives them, Imogen is driven by desperate straits into hers. She wears, as we shall see, her cap and hose with a difference. It is a difference, I shall argue, which requires for its understanding a radical departure in critical method.

According to Johnson's magisterial opinion:

> This play has many just sentiments, some natural dialogues, and some pleasing scenes, but they are obtained at the expense of much incongruity. To remark the folly of the fiction, the absurdity of the conduct, the confusion of the names and manners of different times, and the impossibility of the events in any system of life, were to waste criticism upon unresisting imbecility, upon faults too evident for detection, and too gross for aggravation. ((1756) 1958, 8, 908)

Traditional criticism has not found it easy to circumvent Johnson's rugged rationalism, has indeed very often negotiated itself into culs-de-sac in the attempt. Nosworthy, for instance, pointing out that Johnson failed to take into account the romance genre of the play, in terms of which Johnson's defects are "among the prime virtues" ((1955) 1980, xlviii) finds himself lauding the "symbolic" or schematic characters (the Queen, Cloten, Belarius and the boys, Cymbeline himself) as "the achievement" of Shakespeare's object, namely, "to create characters flattened, insulated, idealized, and unreal, who belong to no normal system of life, but to a world of romance" (1vi), while in consequence the greater realism of Posthumus, Imogen and Iachimo is found to be out of place. Valiantly fighting a rearguard action over the awkward three, Nosworthy dismisses Iachimo as no more than "a stock figure" (1vii), finds Posthumus "one of the dullest of Shakespeare's heroes," who "never really comes to life" (1ix), and Imogen, who "defeated

Shakespeare's intentions by coming to life," "sadly out of character in this play." She is, he says, "enchanting in her cumulative effect," though "a various and erratic tissue of inconsistencies" upon analysis (lxi). It is no wonder then, that criticism thus wound in its own toils "has sometimes had to own itself confounded when it has asked why Shakespeare fashioned the play as he did, or even why he fashioned it at all" (xi). The answer is found in the appeal to a transcendent anagoge which will absolve the play of the defects just attributed to it. Thus *Cymbeline* is not to be regarded (as is customary) "as an oddly unaccountable lapse" in the Shakespearean *oeuvre* but as one of "his supreme utterances" (lxxviii) and this for the reason that it is "purely Shakespearean in its recognition that life itself is not a coherent pattern . . . but a confused series of experiences, good and evil, grave and gay, momentous and trivial," whose end is a "vision of perfect tranquillity, a partial comprehension of that Peace which passeth all understanding" (lxxix, lxxxiii).

Such a shift of ground is familiar in the criticism of the romances as an alternative to hard-nosed Johnson. Barbara Mowatt urges us to renounce our expectations of rationality and probability, of "syllogism" when we come to the late dramas of Shakespeare, so that we may experience "life in its full complexity – tragic and comic, wonderful and terrible, real and unreal, and as unfathomable as Bottom's dream" (1976, 119). Reginald Foakes invokes "the mysterious operation of a providence not understood by the characters" as the only way to explain "the inconsistencies, contradictions and coincidences of the action," its "dream-like strangeness" and unexpectedness, so that in the end we have "an overall consistent and intelligible dramatic mode" which, "as a whole, is like the action of our own lives" (1971, 117–18).

These positions are really criticism with its back to the wall; certainly with its syllogistic back to the wall. A play is (or should be) logical and lifelike. *Cymbeline* is not logical and lifelike. Therefore it is a special kind of play which is like life. Interestingly enough, both of the critics just quoted speak of dream, of dreamlike features, yet they employ interpretative procedures solely appropriate to discourse rationally ordered, mimetically feasible and obedient to the logic of noncontradiction, of time, place, causality and condition. Suppose we attempt to adapt a hermeneutic of dream analysis, or a model of psychoanalytic discourse for the construing of the "strangenesses," absurdities, coincidences, improbabilities in this play? Suppose we assume that dramatis personae, like personae in dreams may be composite or split figures, doubles or proxies for each other, and that language ambiguous, or evocatively charged or polysemous or conspicuously figured may indeed mean more, or other than it ostensibly says?[2]

Certainly *Cymbeline* is an excellent text with which to test such hypotheses. We will go far to find a better. It is my project in the following pages to argue that the strange, the outlandish, the incredibly coincidental, the absurd, grotesque or uncanny can be read, not as excrescences to be somehow explained away, but as profoundly meaningful. To ape for a moment the structuralist type of terminology, and to launch a companion to rhemes, semes and phonemes, such oddities could perhaps be regarded as "dremes" emerging into the ordinary carriage of the plot and the ordinary behaviour of its agents with their own ulterior and covert messages. It is not important, nor is it possible to determine to what extent the author was conscious of them. It is for the purpose of being able to talk about such messages, without determining their status, that we require the notion of a textual unconscious. It is just because *Cymbeline* is replete with representational anomalies, discords and dissonances, presents us with a medley of melodies and chords diverging and converging in a bewildering polyphony, that it can provide a test case for the value of the concept. The question is can we unbind this text, feel our way toward a unifying, organizing fantasy which we can deduce as having generated the play and which, made conscious, is capable of reanimating in us a corresponding working through process? A hundred years of psychoanalysis have accumulated a vast archive of instances analogous to the adventures of our protagonists, and provided a lexicon, but it will not be a matter of deciphering a code or of diagnosing a neurosis in a dramatic character. It is rather a matter of feeling our way into a state of mind, or states of mind, in which the oddities and discrepancies suddenly "figure"; it is a matter, to add a significant letter to Lacan's dictum, of discovering "the 'unsaid' that lies in the (w)holes of the discourse (1977, 93)."

In the first instance this entails psychological analysis, at whatever level, of the motivations and dispositions of the play's protagonists. "What does Imogen (or Posthumus, or Cymbeline) want?" is a primary question, but we at once become aware that it is less important to inquire what, for instance, Iachimo or Cloten or Belarius want, than to figure out what they represent within the imagined worlds of the protagonists. Just as dreams are always about the dreamer, so there is always a central ego for a play to be about. It was precisely the reversal of this hierarchy which was witty and intriguing in Tom Stoppard's *Rosencrantz and Guildenstern are Dead*.

Our first oddity, then, is the play's eponym. Why is the drama named for King Cymbeline, when it is not in any strict sense a history play conventionally named after a reigning monarch, and when he himself, save for his initial banishment of Posthumus, is a passive figure, browbeaten and henpecked by his wicked Queen and incomparably less prominent in the play's action than his sorely tried daughter? About her importance there will no doubt be little argument. The Imogenolatry of nineteenth-century Shakespeare criticism,[3] its roots in defensive Victorian (and Renaissance) idealization to which we no longer subscribe, is still pervasive in the criticism as witness to her centrality, however we may wish to account for it. Yet the King is the pivot and cynosure of all the revelations and recognitions in Act V, suddenly a rival epicentre. The virtual absence of His Majesty the King in the play which is named for him is thus a signifier which demands attention. I believe that the central ego in *Cymbeline* is, ultimately, Cymbeline, but that, for reasons which will presently appear, that ego is in abeyance, in temporary suspension, as it were, behind the three plots through which *Cymbeline* unfolds.

The three plots in *Cymbeline*: the individual marital (Imogen and Posthumus); the familial (the kidnapped brothers); and the national (the rebellion of a province against the Empire) are interlocked with a craft which it is customary to admire; but it is worth noticing that they do not conduct themselves in the least in the way Shakespearean subplots usually do. We are accustomed to three- or even four-tier mirroring structures, as in *A Midsummer Night's Dream*, or *As You Like It*, or *Henry IV*, where goings-on at the socially lower, or more "foolish" levels counterpoint or comment upon the doings and sayings at the upper level.[4] In *Cymbeline* there is no such ramification or hierarchy. Rather there seem to be issues which find expression over and over again, and so suggest the existence of an obsessive need, a compulsion. The play is like a jigsaw puzzle whose broken-apart and mixed-up pieces must be matched and put together. It is like its families. Children are orphaned, or kidnapped, parents bereaved, a wife and husband separated, siblings parted. The confederation of an empire and its province disrupted. Fragmentation is brought to a phantasmagoric extreme; even bodies are dismembered and not recognized. It is worth noticing that the word "thing" as an epithet applied to persons – "Thou basest thing" (I.i.125), "O disloyal thing" (131), "This imperceiverant thing" (IV.i.14), "Slight thing of Italy" (V.iv.64), for instance, occurs in *Cymbeline* more often than in any other of Shakespeare's plays. Notice, in contradistinction to this reification, Posthumus' culminating organic image when he finds himself and Imogen: "Hang there like fruit, my soul," (V.v.263). The personae, disassociated parts of dismembered families, do not recognize each other, or themselves, are confused about their roles, their "parts," especially Posthumus and Imogen. Or else they are partial persons, clearly projective. The Queen is a poison mother, a projection of infantile fantasy. The King is a *nom du père*, a *non du père*, to borrow Lacan's extraordinarily apt witticism, but in his absence other father figures keep springing up. The recognition scenes at the end, until the very last, are partial, piecemeal, kaleidoscopic; people are, and are not, recognized. The King finds Lucius' page, his daughter, hauntingly familiar. Posthumus sees, though he does not recognize, in the feminine beauty of Belarius' sons the resemblance to their sister, his wife. The family, Meredith Skura notes, "is so important that characters cannot even imagine themselves without one" (1980, 205). Their problem, however, is how to imagine themselves within one. Hence, in the course of the drama, families keep being reconstituted, partly, or by proxy, in caves, in visions, in disguise.

Let us pursue the fortunes of the initially presented protagonists. We shall not reach the deepest level of fantasy until we have worked through the more manifest meanings and motivations which lead us to what they screen. But it is to the young lovers that the play first solicits our attention.

The story of Posthumus Leonatus, a fatherless youth whose very name orphans him, is the *Bildungsroman* of a young man whose manhood is under inspection. He is of noble lineage but cannot, as yet, be "delve[d] to the root" (1.i.28). He is put to the test first of all by the banishment which immediately follows his marriage. Skura is wrong when she says that Posthumus' first mistake is to "usurp his proper place" (in his foster family) "when he elopes with Imogen" (1980, 209). He precisely does not elope with her. He allows himself to be separated from her and leaves her in virtual imprisonment in Britain. The Gentleman who lavishes praise upon him, expressing, he says, the general view, announces that he is a creature such

> As, to seek through the regions of the earth
> For one his like, there would be something failing
> In him that should compare   (I.i.20–2)

The syntax is disorientingly ambiguous. Anyone like him would, by virtue of the likeness, possess a failing? Anyone assuming to be compared with him would, by virtue of the comparison, be found wanting? We settle, of course for the second, but we cannot quite rid our minds of the other possibility the syntax and lineation allows. This is followed by a very curious phrase in the Gentleman's assurance to his interlocuter that he is not exaggerating:

I do extend him, sir, within himself,
Crush him together rather than unfold
His measure duly.   (25–7)

This suggests some malleable object rather than the admired
scion of a noble stock; and we learn, in Pisanio's account of
Cloten's attack upon him, that "My master rather play'd than
fought/And had no help of anger" (I.i.161–3). What are we
being told, in so devious a manner, about Posthumus the
universally praised? Some doubts about the "eagle" quality of
Imogen's lover must surely enter one's mind, the more
especially since her own defiance of her father has been
outspoken and unequivocal. Interestingly enough, his own
first words to his beloved betray a self-consciousness about the
very question of manliness:

My queen, my mistress!
O lady, weep no more, lest I give cause
To be suspected of more tenderness
Than doth become a man.   (I.i.92–5)

These two newly-wed quasi-siblings, violently separated,
their marriage unconsummated, mark their parting with the
gift of significantly symbolic transitional objects. She gives
him a diamond, her mother's, to be parted with only after her
death, when he will woo her successor; he, invoking death
rather than such a possibility, "imprisons" her arm with a
bracelet, a "manacle of love" (122). He needs to "possess" her
(his preoccupation with possessions is evident throughout),
and is uncertain of his tenure. She needs to foster and cherish
him, but, as we touchingly learn when she relives, with
Pisanio, the distancing of his ship, worrying about getting
letters, reimagining his diminishing image, envying the hand-
kerchief he kissed and waved, mourning the lost opportunity
to bask in a lover's appreciation, she needs him as a mirror in
which she can see herself, recognize herself as cherished and
valued.

I did not take my leave of him, but had
Most pretty things to say. Ere I could tell him

How I would think on him at certain hours . . .
                    or I could make him swear
The shes of Italy should not betray
Mine interest and his honor . . .
                              or ere I could
Give him that parting kiss which I had set
Betwixt two charming words, comes in my father,
And like the tyrannous breathing of the north
Shakes all our buds from growing.   (I.iii.25–37, passim)

They are buds in their youthfulness, in their youthful
narcissism, and they are "shaken" from growing by the
blocking father that Cymbeline is to them. Buds that are kept
from growing together, grow apart, revealing fatal dissonances
in their relationship, and disequilibrium in their personalities.

That Posthumus allowed himself to be torn from his bride,
did not snatch her to him and take flight with her, is, of course,
a donnée of the play; but much, and with a certain emphasis, is
made of it. In Act II, scene iv Philario asks Posthumus what
means he is taking to overcome the King's interdict. "Not
any," is the reply,

                    but abide the change of time,
Quake in the present winter's state, and wish
That warmer days would come.   (4–6)

This is followed by an oxymoron which reads suspiciously like
a slip of the tongue. "In these fear'd hopes," says Posthumus, "I
barely gratify your love" (6–7). Which emotion, if any, is
dominant? fear, hope, doubt? If it is felt that pessimism or
trepidation is sufficiently accounted for by a state of fatherless-
ness, propertylessness and banishment, it is worth recalling
that Imogen refers to him "when he was here" as "inclin[ing]
to sadness, and oft-times/Not knowing why" (I.vi.61–3) and
that the sigh that escapes her: "O, that husband!/My supreme
crown of grief. . . . Had I been thief-stol'n,/As my two brothers,
happy!" (3–6), makes her cause of grief anaphorically her
husband himself rather than, or at least as well as, his absence;
and while it ostensibly refers to the stealing away of her
brothers in the past, contains the suggestion of a wished-for

stealing away of herself in the present. Posthumus, who speaks very highly of his countrymen as formidable warriors, lacks himself, it seems, sufficient pugnacity to shine as a lover, and it is as a chivalric lover that he is put to the test in Rome by the challenge of a mischief-making Italian.

There is much to be learned from the provocation scene. First of all it is not, evidently, the first such occasion, but a repetition of a similar chivalric affirmation of the superlative virtue of a lady, which would have ended at sword's point save for the intervention of the Frenchman. Iachimo, subtle manipulator, who has already disparaged Posthumus before his entrance, sets his trap cunningly. The target of his cynicism is first of all Woman. British women, and Posthumus' "unparagon'd mistress" (80) are simply specific instances of the general law. "I make my wager rather against your confidence than her reputation . . . I durst attempt it against any lady in the world" (110–13); but his barbs are personal, pointed and belittling and leave Posthumus little alternative than the mandatory chivalric response. "You may wear her in title yours; but you know strange fowl light upon neighbouring ponds" (88–9); "With five times so much conversation, I should get ground of your fair mistress" (103–4); "If you buy ladies' flesh at a million a dram, you cannot preserve it from tainting. But I see you have some religion in you, that you fear" (134–7).

There is no question about the provocation. The question that the scene raises is Posthumus' response. For what is, after all, the expected knightly procedure? Surely in such circumstances a man would challenge the slanderer, even the mere doubter of his mistress's honour, to a duel without further ado. It is himself, as against his adversary, that he would put to the test, not his inviolate lady. The scene itself reminds us of this in its reference to the previous occasion, and Philario, nervously attempting to allay the tension: "Let us leave here, gentlemen" (99), "Gentlemen, enough of this. It came in too suddenly; let it die as it was born, and I pray you be better acquainted" (120–2), has clearly such an outcome in mind. Instead of the "the arbiterment of swords" (49), however, we have the taking of the wager, which places the onus of proof upon the lady, and makes Posthumus' manly honor dependent, not upon an action of his, but upon an action, or nonaction, of hers. If Imogen prove faithless, "I am no further your enemy; she is not worth our debate" (159–60); but the whole chivalric point, surely, is to maintain at sword's point his *belief* in her faithfulness! If she is faithful, *then* he will punish Iachimo – "you shall answer me with your sword" (163). Both these alternatives take refuge in male bonds and relations in which, it seems, Posthumus shelters. The wager makes Imogen a mere object through which a bond with Iachimo is cemented: either he will become his friend, no woman between them, or his chastiser, again man to man. The wager reflects an inner question, the possibility of which the text has already insinuated into our minds: shall be (can he?) be a man among men, or a man to a woman?

If Iachimo finds her unassailable, and so not only of supreme worth but also manifestly devoted to Posthumus, this will flatter Posthumus' self-esteem; but what if the cunning, cynical Italian succeeds in gaining possession of "her dearest bodily part" (150), in performing, in other words, as Posthumus' proxy? Does the wager (rather than a duel) fulfill some inner need or desire of Posthumus himself? Is there a secret complicity between inveigler and inveigled?

What for that matter, if Cloten, master of all he surveys in England, gets possession of Imogen? These two are both assailants upon Imogen's chastity, would-be performers of her lover's role, and they are diametrically opposed, sophisticated, cunning, gallant and coarse lout, Queen's son though he be. They are clearly antithetical doubles. If there is an element of cultural comment in the mimetic aspect of their representation – English provincial against Italianate rogue – this remains marginal in the play as a whole. On the other hand the antithesis resonates throughout the whole play and acquires an organizing force when we can see it as in some way significantly related to Posthumus himself. Such a relation has been proposed by Murray Schwartz, building skillfully upon Freud's analysis of "The Universal Tendency to Debasement in the Sphere of Love."

Iachimo and Cloten, he says, "represent two related obsessions of a Renaissance personality burdened with the idealization and worship of women and seeking to establish a stable relationship between platonic sublimation and crude sexual expression." Both are "aspects or projections of Posthumus' psyche" which is "in tense and precarious balance" between alternative sexual modes (1976, 231). "By following Posthumus carefully through the play we can identify the dreamlike logic (the logic of displacement, condensation, substitution, multiple symbolization) which underlies its sometimes confusing, over-sophisticated surface," and discover in him "the tyranny of the superego which would split the psyche into diametric opposites, one part that worships and another that defiles" (236).

We can interpret the play's psychomachia, then, as an inhibition of desire on Posthumus' part which is exhibited in extremely subtle ways through the two proxy suitors, the fastidious Iachimo and the unspeakable Cloten. The following account of this representation of inner conflict owes much to Schwartz' explication, though I do not follow him completely, either in detail or in respect to his conclusions.[5]

Cloten is introduced as early as Act I, scene ii in all his gross, rank, brute libidinality. Pretending to machismo, he is derided by his attendant lords with a flattery the irony of which is so palpable that only a Cloten-fool could miss it. We meet him again immediately before the bedroom scene, when his malodorous presence and his phallic/martial non-exploits are called attention to: "a pox on't! I had rather not be so noble as I am. They dare not fight with me because of the Queen my mother. Every Jack slave hath his bellyful of fighting, and I must go up and down like a cock that nobody can match" (II.i.18–22). Cloten, says Murray Schwartz, is "unadulterable phallic aggression" (1976, 222), a "personification of infantile fixations" (226); "Cloten represents . . . uncontrolled phallic wishes that seek their objects relentlessly and without the least regard for otherness" (223). However, Cloten's sexuality is not sheer animal lust, or uninhibited libido. It is disowned by a constant defensive meiosis. The lexis with which he is associated is drawn from a "south-fog" (II.iii.131) of cloacal, noisome and obscene imagery. As Schwartz puts it, "He embodies the belief that sexuality defiles its object and drags chastity through the mire" (225). Cloten and Iachimo are not simply two rival evils laying siege to Imogen's integrity and virtue, but secret sharers in the psyche of the absent Post-humus for whom they substitute, and it is this that gives the two personae and the psychomachia they articulate its particular depth and interest. Both Cloten and his counterpart Iachimo ("Cloten in civilised dress," as Schwartz puts it, 227) represent isolated and split-off parts of an ambivalent and unintegrated personality, the one "arrogant piece of flesh," pure sexual drive, "the rebellion of a codpiece" (225); the other, pure, aim-inhibited fantasy as exhibited in the exquisite aestheticism of the bedroom scene.

Cloten, intent upon serenading the object of his desire, is nakedly lewd: "I am advis'd to give her music a'mornings; they say it will penetrate. . . . If you can penetrate her with your fingering, so; we'll try with tongue too" (II.iii.11–15). The aubade opens the scene which follows Iachimo's bedroom visit. The contrast could hardly be more extreme. The aubade is itself readable "from above" and "from below": as pretty Ovidian myth or, through its flying, its rising, its steeds watering at the springs of chaliced flowers, its winking Mary-buds that begin to ope their eyes, as veiled coitus. It is ironic in that no night of love has in fact been enjoyed; but it sharpens our perception that in fantasy one indeed has. The "fingering" and "tonguing" of Cloten has its marvelously imagined counterpart in Iachimo's soliloquy at Imogen's bedside.

Iachimo's virtuoso performance at his first meeting with Imogen gives us notice of his talent for verbalizing fantasy, for enlisting primary process imagery in the eliciting of sexual excitement:

> Had I this cheek
> To bathe my lips upon; this hand, whose touch
> (Whose every touch) would force the feeler's soul

To th'oath of loyalty; this object, which
Takes prisoner the wild motion of mine eye,
Firing it only here; should I (damn'd then)
Slaver with lips as common as the stairs
That mount the Capitol   (I.vi.99–106)

Somatic evocations of bodily sensations and excitations, are aroused and disclaimed by the careful web of denigration of Posthumus and the "shes" that, he insinuates, Posthumus is "vaulting" in Rome: the sluts, the tomboys, the boiled stuff, the garbage that "Should make desire vomit emptiness,/Not so allured to feed" (45–6). It is the rhetoric of a maestro, but whom is it persuading? The audience is in the know at this point and must experience a species of split response, being partly persuaded as a real Imogen might have been persuaded, and partly persuaded only of the virtuousity of Iachimo. This means that the rhetoric itself is an object of attention and not a transparent medium, that the textuality (or fictionality) of the characters is not for a moment forgotten. This is an important point because it is what enables us to move about within the fictional space from one implied consciousness, or uncon-sciousness, to another.

We have no way of knowing whether his climatic ploy:

                              Should he make me
Live, like Diana's priest, betwixt cold sheets,
Whiles he is vaulting variable ramps,
In your despite, upon your purse – revenge it.
I dedicate myself to your sweet pleasure   (132–6)

is an inadvertant overreaching from which he adroitly extri-cates himself, or a part of his manipulative strategy. Nor can we know whether the trunk trick is a brilliant improvisation or, again, the culminating move in a premeditated masterplan; but we know that we are watching a game of cat and mouse. Nevertheless we are as manipulated as Imogen, who rejoices to take the trunk of jewels associated with Posthumus into the protection of her very bedchamber; we are as surprised as she would have been had she awoken, when Iachimo steps out of the trunk. The impact of the stage effect is therefore extremely shocking and partakes of that moment of disorientation often experienced upon waking from a dream when one is not yet able to distinguish between the oneiric and the real. It is as if the distancing fictional frame had collapsed and Iachimo is suddenly "real," really there or real in our minds, and this undoubtedly plays its part in creating the peculiarly intense effect of the passage which follows.

Iachimo would rather poison Posthumus' mind than possess Imogen's body. So he does not touch her. He denies himself the kiss which he projects onto the "rubies unparagoned" of her lips: "How dearly they do't!" (II.ii.17–18). "Doing," however, is far more than kissing in the imagery which follows. If we allow the language to work its will upon us we will perceive how Iachimo savors every moment of a fantasized sexual act. He begins with the invocation of Tarquin, relishing the latter's menacing tread: "Our Tarquin thus/Did softly press the rushes ere he waken'd/The chastity he wounded" (12–14). Desire is concentrated in an intensity of seeing, a lust of the eyes. The phallic flame of the taper is itself a voyeur as it "Bows toward her, and would under-peep her lids" (19–20); the bracelet (an upward displacement) is removed with ease – it is "As slippery as the Gordian knot was hard" (34); the climax, which has brought so many empathetic critics to a similar exalted state, engages a number of primal desires in its minutely observed image. The "crimson drops/I'th' bottom of a cowslip" (38–9), defloration in an innocently pastoral mask, is transferred to the mole upon her breast, redoubling fantasied pleasure. The soliloquy closes with an orgasm – a rape – completed: "the leaf's turn'd down/Where Philomel gave up" (45–6), and Iachimo, brought out of his trance by the striking clock (51), returns to the trunk with a gnawing sense of guilt.

Iachimo shrewdly exploits vicarious fantasy when he returns with his report, first of her bedchamber "where I confess I slept not" (II.iv.67), with its tapestry of Cleopatra "when she met her Roman/And Cydnus swelled above the banks" (70–1), its chimney piece of "Chaste Dian bathing" (81–2), its winking Cupid andirons, and finally the mole in its "delicate lodging"

beneath her breast, which, he says, he kissed, to the enhance-
ment of an appetite just sated (137–8). Posthumus is sexually
aroused by the account. His bitter "Spare your arithmetic,
never count the turns" (142) is vividly obscene, as is the
tell-tale condensation of images in the rosy "pudency" (is the
lady blushing? or is the sweet view another rosy site?) in his
succeeding soliloquy:

> Me of my lawful pleasure she restrain'd
> And pray'd me oft forbearance; did it with
> A pudency so rosy the sweet view on't
> Might well have warm'd old Saturn, that I thought her
> As chaste as unsunn'd snow.   (II.v.9–13)

Just as he "sees" that rosy "pudency" so he "sees" the
"full-acorned" boar which "Cried 'O!' and mounted" (16–17),
an image in which high feeding and high sexuality coalesce
under the pressure of the imagined scene.

Posthumus, we perceive, is precipitated into his Cloten self,
his unreconstructed, for him demeaning sensuality, by Iachimo's machinations. The bracelet is a basilisk – a Medusa's
head – that kills him to look on; the metonymic mole a "stain,
as big as hell can hold" (II.iv.140); and in savage reaction he
will "tear her limb-meal!" (147), obliterating, in his misogynis-
tic outburst, the threat, and magnet, that is "the woman's
part" (II.v.20). "The woman's part" is, in analytic terminology,
overdetermined. It is the "dearest bodily part" which his
exacerbated fantasy has "seen"; it is the maternal half of
procreation which he would repudiate: "Is there no way for
men to be, but women/Must be half-workers?" (1–2) and upon
which he projects all falsities and evils, including his own
sense of inauthenticity: his father was, must have been, absent
when he "was stamped," when "some coiner with his
tools/Made [him] a counterfeit" (5); and it is, as the woman's
part in him – sex, his own repressed sexuality, his own fear of
sexual inadequacy, his sexual jealousy – for which he blames
women and from which he recoils in rage:

> I'll write against them,
> Detest them, curse them, yet 'tis greater skill
> In a true hate to pray they have their will:
> The very devils cannot plague them better. (32–5)

Finally, in the letter which informs Pisanio that "Thy mistress . . . hath play'd the strumpet in my bed" (III.iv.21–2), Posthumus, in a perverse, self-contaminating turn, incorporates the woman's part. "Thy mistress hath play'd the strumpet in my bed: the testimonies whereof lies bleeding in me." It is he who is the violated virgin since he cannot be the violator that in his present sexual violence he would wish to be.

To illuminate the play's psychomachia from the side of the triad Posthumus, Iachimo, Cloten, however, is to default on half the story. There is another side to the inner conflict in Act II which is plotted through the opposite aspect of the triangle – Imogen, Iachimo, Cloten. The relations can be diagramed:

Iachimo
Imogen   Posthumus
Cloten

These symmetries invite assessment of the protagonists as mirror images of each other. Both are ideal objects to each other; both are victims; both take flight and both seek rehabilitation (literally) in other clothing; and not only Posthumus, but also Imogen, we very soon discover, is in subtle tension or disharmony with her sexuality.

We may have already noticed that Imogen, the fiercely rejected daughter ("Nay, let her languish/A drop of blood a day, and being aged/Die of this folly!" (I.i.156–8)) of a possessive father, chafes at the constraints of being a woman. Hearing of the near-fight between Posthumus and Cloten she says,

> I would they were in Afric both together,
> Myself by with a needle, that I might prick
> The goer-back.   (167–9)

This is odd considering that the "goer-back," according to

Pisanio, was Posthumus himself, and therefore betrays a certain vexation in this abandoned bride. Her reference to her husband as "My supreme crown of grief ... Had I been thief-stol'n,/As my two brothers, happy!" (I.vi.4–6) has already been noted (see p. 71). Imogen is ardent and loving, and not about to admit to any defect in her beloved, but her tongue betrays her.

She is herself hard-pressed. Not only does she remain alone, in virtual imprisonment, in the absence of her lover, beset by the coarse lout she detests as much as she detests his mother, but she is verbally assaulted by the man who comes to her as her husband's friend.

We note her spirited resistance to Iachimo's innuendos in the testing scene, and her repudiation of him when he gives himself away; but it is his giveaway that has saved her. "My lord, I fear,/Has forgot Britain" (I.vi.112–13) she has just said, dismayed despite herself. It is this perhaps that accounts for the eagerness with which, appeased by Iachimo's retraction, she takes the trunk into custody into her own bedchamber. However, there is, we are invited to infer, another reason. The precious trunk contains jewels purchased by Posthumus: its contents stand therefore, as nearly as any object may, for his bodily presence. It is both in longing and to make amends that she wishes it so close.

Imogen, in the bedroom scene, is an inert, sleeping presence, the object of Iachimo's fantasy, but the references to time which set off and frame Iachimo's soliloquy, mark off a timeless space of fantasy, or dream, for Imogen too. She has been reading for three hours, we learn, before she falls asleep. She prays for protection, as she puts her book aside, from "fairies and the tempters of the night" (II.ii.9); and when we discover at what episode her reading terminated – in the tale of Tereus, "where Philomel gave up" (46) – we can see why. Wedded, but unbedded, abandoned, in effect, by her husband, her marriage proscribed and herself rejected by her father, beset like Penelope by unwanted suitors, the story of Philomel and Tereus objectifies ambivalent fear and excitement.

In the next scene she is the victim of Cloten's gross

attentions, no less unsettling than were Iachimo's crafty
manipulations. She has also lost her bracelet. So, understandably, at Cloten's curse, "The south-fog rot him!" (II.iii.131),
she momentarily loses her composure; but her vehement
comparison is more expressive than perhaps she, the imagined
persona, is aware:

> His mean'st garment
> That ever hath but clippt his body, is dearer
> In my respect than all the hairs above thee,
> Were they all made such men.   (133–6)

What is a man's meanest garment? The train of thought picks
up from Cloten's talk about Posthumus' "beggary," but the
train of feeling, we intuit, arises elsewhere. This garment
"clippt his body." A man's homely underwear could presumably fit the bill as his meanest garment, and it is also that
which "clips" his body closest. Read thus, the otherwise
entirely obscure leap to Cloten's tonsorial style (or wig?)
becomes explicable. The displacement upwards of the body-
image is a protection from the recognition, which it also
divulges, of a lively desire. Just such a displacement, common
in dream language, this time from sexual to aural penetration
occurs in her response to Pisanio's embassy: "Speak thick/
(Love's counsellor should fill the bores of hearing,/To th'
smothering of the sense) . . . Tell me how Wales was made so
happy as/T' inherit such a haven" (III.ii.56–62, passim). Her
mingling of ardour, impatience and trepidation, touching in
itself, is given a further dimension when we take in the deeper
resonances.

Cloten, thick-witted in all but his own monolithic concerns,
gets the humiliating point about the clothes, as is made clear
in the sequel when he sends for Posthumus' clothes in which
he will pursue the pair to Milford Haven:

> Even there, thou villain Posthumus, will I kill thee. . . . She
> said upon a time (the bitterness of it I now belch from my
> heart) that she held the very garment of Posthumus in more
> respect than my noble and natural person, together with the

adornment of my qualities. With that suit upon my back will I ravish her; first kill him, and in her eyes; there shall she see my valor, which will then be a torment to her contempt. He on the ground, my speech of insultment ended on his dead body, and when my lust hath din'd (which, as I say, to vex her I will execute in the clothes that she so praised) to the court I'll knock her back, foot her home again. (III.v.131–46, passim)

"O for a horse with wings!" Imogen says, when Posthumus' letter summons her to Milford Haven (III.ii.48). And when Pisanio assures her that they can cover no more than a score of miles "twixt sun and sun" (68): "Why, one that rode to's execution, man,/Could never go so slow" (70–1). This is patent dramatic irony, of course. Pisanio has already read Posthumus' murder letter, and Imogen will hear of it before she gets to her heaven-haven; but if nothing is accidental in the world of the mind then the uttering of such a comparison must indicate the presence of an underlying dread. The manner in which this passionate and high-spirited girl – who has defied her father's fury, who struggles, alone, to resolve the ambivalence of untried sexuality, suffering the absence of her lover with some accusatory vexation, however unacknowledged – responds to the outrage of her husband's misconception of her becomes thus poignantly understandable:

> False to his bed? What is it to be false?
> To lie in watch there and to think on him?
> To weep 'twixt clock and clock? If sleep charge nature,
> To break it with a fearful dream of him,
> And cry myself awake?   (III.iv.40–4)

Outraged and bewildered, her defense against his accusations takes the form of an accusatory injury against herself: she begs Pisanio to kill her – to do his master's bidding – with an image of mutilation, of positive dismemberment:

> Poor I am stale, a garment out of fashion,
> And for I am richer than to hang by th' walls,
> I must be ripp'd. To pieces with me! (51–3)

This is a turning inward of her anger and her anguish. She sees herself a hunted or trapped creature, a sacrificial lamb or deer, turns feminine sexual submission into masochistic punishment as she tosses away the protective wad of Posthumus' letters in her bosom and invites the sword's penetration: "Obedient as the scabbard" (80). Her first defense against the mortification of Posthumus' treatment of her is a literal mortifying of herself – a mort of the deer, so to speak.

However, Imogen, possessed of remarkable resilience, recovers. Even before Pisanio's suggestion of the page disguise, she has taken heart, and determined, in the first place, not to return to the court:

No court, no father, nor no more ado
With that harsh, noble, simple nothing,
That Cloten, whose love suit hath been to me
As fearful as a siege. . . .
Hath Britain all the sun that shines? day? night?
Are they not but in Britain?　　(131–7)

Her response to her plight, like Posthumus' to his, but with opposite effect, is also to reject "the woman's part" in her, to "forget to be a woman" (154). She embraces Pisanio's idea of the journey to Italy with enthusiasm, is "almost a man already" (166–7), and will "abide it with a prince's courage" (183–4); but Imogen's transvestite fantasy solves nothing.

First of all, footsore and weary, she discovers that "a man's life is a tedious one" (III.vi.1), as she remarks with a wry humor. However, it is her hermaphrodite membership in the reconstituted family of Belarius which makes clear that her flight from her sex will never do. Not only is her real sex only partly concealed – the brothers clearly fall in love with the feminine quality of her beauty (much as does Orsino with Cesario's): "Were you a woman, youth,/I should woo hard" (68–9) – but also the family likeness between the three is, we infer, only partly concealed. Unavailable to conscious knowledge it is evidently unconsciously registered. For Imogen the vigorous masculinity of the peerless twain is extremely attractive but what it precipitates is a wishful fantasy about her lost brothers, which she invokes to mitigate the defaulting of Posthumus. "Would . . . they/Had been my father's sons" (75–6) she thinks, for then, no longer sole heiress to her father's crown (nor sole object of his possessive love) – her "prize" would have been less and so "more equal ballasting" to Posthumus, and their love might have fared better (76–7). As it is, rejected and calumniated she reaffirms that she would rather be a man in their company than a woman to the false Leonatus.

The audience, knowing what it knows, perceives this encounter synoptically. What is (and is not) being recognized by the brothers is Imogen's true gender. What is not (and yet is) being recognized by all three is their kinship. The love which springs up between them is therefore a composite of elements: narcissistic, erotic and familial, a volatile quantity which cannot recognize itself or disentangle its objects.

The rural retreat in Wales is the "green world" or other place which in Shakespearean comedy is liberating and restorative;[6] but it *is* a retreat – from maturation; a return to infancy, or even beyond, to the shelter of a cave/womb. Belarius is a mother/father – he was a tree "whose boughs did bend with fruit" until the "storm or robbery" which "shook down [his] mellow hangings . . . and left [him] bare to weather" (III.iii.61–4). The siblings are androgynous, or sexless – Fidele sings like an angel, and cooks like one too; they all, in fact, cook and keep house like women, though the boys are hunters too. This denial of adult differentiation is, on the one hand, gratifying, healing, a wishful undoing, but the play keeps a stern and monitoring eye on it.

The retreat is glossed in the homilies of Belarius as a beneficient exchange of the sophistries and corruptions of the court for the archaic simplicities of nature, and his contempt for the gates of monarchs, which are "arched so high that giants may jet through/And keep their impious turbands on without/Good morrow to the sun" (5–7), is a detraction of masculine arrogance. It is subverted by the aspiration of the boys to live the life of the "full-winged eagle" rather than that of the "sharded beetle" (20–1), and by Belarius' own approval of their "wild" violence, which he sees as evidence of an "invisible instinct" of royalty (IV.ii.177ff). They are precariously poised, in their immaturity, between the noble and the savage; and, all unawares, between innocence and incest since the eruption into their lives of Fidele. The Belarius family romance – designed to "bar [the king] of succession" (III.iii.102) – represents a barren wish. Belarius' is a fantasy family whose childlike nondifferentiation is regressive.

Back at the British court sexual roles are also, in their own way, fruitlessly and damagingly inverted. Cymbeline is patently reluctant to rise against the imperial father figure Caesar, who knighted him and under whom he spent his youth. Patriotic self-assertion is left to the Queen and her son, whose joint monopolization of the masculine virtues is rendered in interestingly characteristic ways. Cloten, crude as ever, announces that "we will nothing pay/For wearing our own noses" (III.i.13–14). The Queen describes the British isles as a *hortus inclusus* ("Neptune's park," within its "salt-water girdle" in Cloten's description (80)), a space normally feminine in the symbology of landscapes, but here fortified and lethal:

> ribb'd and pal'd in
> With oaks unscalable and roaring waters,
> With sands that will not bear your enemies' boats,
> But suck them up to th' topmast.   (19–22)

Britain's heirs, cavemen in Wales, are mothered by a man, Britain itself is kinged by a woman, who, if she has her way and her wish for the speedy demise of both Imogen and her father, will soon in fact "have the placing of the British crown" upon her son's head (III.v.65). The play's central Act has brought the drama to an imminent crisis of intrigue at court, and war over the tribute money. In Belarius' other isle Cloten closes in upon the fugitive Imogen. Appropriately, at the outset of Act IV Fidele, succumbing to grief for her lost love, falls ill.

In Shakespearean tragic structure we regularly find protagonists in Act IV facing a great void, an annihilation of the values which have sustained them. Deprived of their objects of love or faith or hope, they experience despair, so that possible remedy, tantalizingly just within reach, is occluded from their view, or, if perceived, is snatched away by the circumstances which have swept beyond control. In his comic structures, Act IV initiates the remedial phase of the narrative, exorcizing precedent errors and follies by maximilizing them to the point of exhaustion. In *Cymbeline*, the most intricately interlocked of the tragicomedies, both vectors coexist, and are synchronized in the play's most phantasmagoric event – the mock death of Fidele. In terms of form the bizarre and lurid events in Wales mark the concatenation of the two contradictory genres in a grotesque indeterminacy of tragic and comic effects. In terms of fantasy they mark a turning point in the working through of the deep conflicts the play articulates.

Imogen, heartsick, takes the potion given her by Pisanio in the belief that it is remedial, which it is, the malignant will of the Queen having been outwitted by Cornelius, her physician, who exchanged her poisonous brew for a harmless narcotic. Only Cornelius, however, knows this. It enables the tragicomic transformation of grave and serious events into restorative and gratifying ends. Had it been the poison the Queen intended it to be, Imogen's taking it, on advice from the good Pisanio, would have constituted the fatal error in a tragic sequence of ironic reversals and disasters. As it is, it constitutes the mock deception which brings about a sequence of harmless (though painful) errors, mistaken identities and confusions, which will issue, despite the harm already caused, in a benign resolution. It is the cause of the (apparent) death which the play, as comedy, will surmount, while at the same time it is the cause that the death *is* only apparent, a deathlike trance. It thus provides for a playing out and working through, in imagination, of the despairing or destructive urge which drags against the play's reconstructive thrust.

Cloten, hot-foot on Imogen's track, vicious in his retaliatory intent to kill Posthumus, ravish her and spurn her home to her father, is beheaded by Guiderius, and his "clotpole" sent down the stream "in embassy to his mother" (IV.ii.185) in a strange parody of pagan fertility rituals. As a consequence, the Queen, bereft, so to speak, of her male organ, declines and dies. This effectively does away with the evil ones, eliminating sadism and reincorporating it with its primal source, the voracious mother of infantile fantasy.

That Imogen, who was found in bed by Iachimo, is now found in her (death) bed with Cloten, reiterates the relationship of these two to her absent husband: the one representing the repressed libido in him, the other the repressive superego. Posthumus' next appearance, as we shall see, exhibits him with the violent Cloten-id elements in his personality entirely extinguished, and later he will rout Iachimo in single fight; but we shall return to Posthumus' fortunes presently.

In terms of the emotional dynamic of the play it is a melancholy course that is charted by the sequence from bedroom scene to burial scene. In the bedroom scene eroticism was deviant and devious, but alive. The bedroom scene was accompanied by the aubade, an accolade to love; the burial scene by the dirge, which welcomes death. This haunting lyric envisages a sublime indifference to reed as to oak, to both joy and moan, a placid acceptance of the dust to which golden lads and girls must come. Its desire is for death, for the cessation of being and of vicissitude, a "quiet consummation" devoutly to be wished. However, Imogen wakes bewildered from her drugged stupor to discover the headless body of Cloten/Posthumus beside her. "Limb-meal" she inventories her lover's body:

> I know the shape of's leg; this is his hand,
> His foot Mercurial, his Martial thigh,
> The brawns of Hercules; but his Jovial face –
> Murther in heaven?   (IV.ii.309–12)

Throwing herself upon the faceless, headless body she enacts an hysterical incorporation: she smears her cheek with the blood of the corpse, as if to die herself, or, in a gruesome fantasy realization of Elizabethan "dying," to match her maidenhead with the violated head of her lover.[7] In this "consummation" Eros is undone, overwhelmed, by Thanatos, its dark companion.

"I am nothing; or if not,/Nothing to be were better" (367–8) is Imogen's desolate reply to Lucius' question "What art thou?" (366) when he comes upon the scene at the graveside. It is just here that the countermovement to recovery is initiated. Fidele's head was to be laid to the east, we recall, in preparation, we now perceive, for just such a rebirth. "Wilt take thy chance with me? I will not say/Thou shalt be so well master'd, but be sure/No less belov'd" (382–4), Lucius says, and in response to her vulnerable epicene youthfulness insists that he would "rather father thee than master thee" (395). Imogen, dogged survivor, responds.

Posthumus' progress towards recovery begins with his conscience-stricken, grief-stricken soliloquy at the start of the play's final phase. This is our first meeting with Posthumus since his outburst of misogyny in Act II, scene v. Now he addresses the bloody cloth, evidence, as he believes, of Imogen's death. The great rage is killed in him, and there is a yearning for some form of expression for love, although he is still convinced of Imogen's "wrying":

>   You married ones,
> If each of you should take this course, how many
> Must murther wives much better than themselves
> For wrying but a little! . . . .
>   Gods, if you
> Should have ta'en vengeance on my faults, I never
> Had liv'd to put on this; so had you saved
> The noble Imogen to repent, and strook
> Me, wretch, more worth your vengeance. But alack,
> You snatch some hence for little faults; that's love,
> To have them fall no more . . .
>   I'll . . .
>   suit myself
> As does a Britain peasant; so I'll fight
> Against the part I come with; so I'll die
> For thee, O Imogen, even for whom my life
> Is every breath a death   (V.i.2–27, passim)

Is there equivocation in "the part I come with" (we recall

"the woman's part in him" so bitterly denounced); it is at all events the sadistic, revengeful Cloten part of him which is here repudiated. Later, he routs Iachimo whose "manhood" has been "taken off" by "the heaviness and guilt within [his] bosom (V.ii.1–2). Neither of the remorseful pair is aware of the other's identity, and there seems little sense, plot-wise, in the dumbshow fight which is superfluous to the conduct of the war and the rescue of the King, the matter at issue at this point in the story. All the more inviting, therefore, is it to see the victory as a symbolic defeat of the Iachimo within.

It is the rescue of the King, however, which serves as focus of the action. It is anticipated by the two boys, given in dumbshow, and then again in Posthumus' vividly detailed account. Three times during the sequence the setting of the heroic feat is described: in a narrow lane (ditched and walled with turf), an old man and two boys (the British forces having retreated in disarray) are defending the King from the oncoming Roman host, when Posthumus joins them. Why the triple insistence? Battle at a narrow entry is, psychoanalytic findings inform us, a classic symbolization of oedipal conflict. In the context of other subliminal recoveries in this phase of the play, the episode reads like an oedipal conflict reversed, or resolved. No father is killed at a crossroads, or maternal portal, but a king is saved, and by his own sons, together with their other (supposed) father, with Posthumus, the unknown soldier, the foster-son, as partner. The text is underscoring its message, but for Posthumus further realizations are necessary before the catastrophic splits in his personality can be truly healed. Isolated, unknown and bereaved, he is still in despair. His oscillating changes of dress from Roman to British signify that he is a man without an identity, rudderless, directionless, deprived of the will to live. Only death offers a surcease to the pain of loss and the agony of conscience; but he cannot find death "where [he] did hear him groan,/Nor feel him where he strook" (V.iii.69–70). The more daringly and fearlessly he fights, the more invulnerable he seems.

When he is captured, therefore, this time in Roman clothing, he welcomes his imprisonment, begging the "good gods" who he welcomes his imprisonment, begging the "good gods" who "coin'd" his life not to extend his torment, not to be "appeased," like "temporal fathers" by his sorrow, and looks forward to his execution with an eagerness which makes the Gaoler remark "Unless a man would marry a gallows and beget young gibbets, I never saw one so prone" (V.iv.198–9). It is at this point that the death-courting Posthumus has a transforming dream.

The departure from blank verse for the dream and the theophany embedded in it have caused much critical agitation[8] which has simply obscured the insight the dream's substance provides into Posthumus' state of mind. The dream, for Posthumus, is a transparent wish-fulfillment. The parental presences which materialize in the dream are solacing, comforting, approving; "our son is good" is the burden of their sayings. He fell asleep grief and guilt stricken, invoking the image of the injured Imogen, craving for the punishment, and the relief, of death. In the dream he is embraced, pitied, exonerated by parents and siblings alike. When he awakes to the pain of the loss of this oneiric family, he is nevertheless imbued with a sense of a "golden chance," of having been "steep'd in favours" (V.iv.131–2); and although he is still absolute for death even after the dream, and unable to interpret the oracular message, the fantasy of recuperation points to its possibility.

Both Imogen and Posthumus thus experience an annihilating despair, their recovery from which is staged in parallel fashion: through the second-chance gift of protective parents. However, their rehabilitation will not be completely realized until the climactic moment of the blow the unrecognized Imogen receives at Posthumus' hand when she intercedes, in order to reveal herself, at the height of his lament for the woman he has wronged and lost. It is a dramatic moment, but it is more than a mere *coup de théâtre*. This acting out of aggression immediately undone by recognition and forgiveness is therapeutic. The blow is an uninhibited action, spontaneous, unconstrained, passionate, and this is a capacity that his masculinity needs as much as her femininity desires. The shock, moreover, functions for both like a clearing of the air, a clearance of debt or a lovers' quarrel, defusing unconscious resentments which could fester and obstruct, functioning to liberate him from his fear of sexual inadequacy, her from her fear of sexual surrender.

What he says as he hits her is pregnant with dramatic irony bred of all the blindnesses there have been between them, and within them:

> Shall's have a play of this? Thou scornful page,
> There lie thy part.   (V.v.228–9)

This is the last time we shall hear that telling little word "part." Fragmentation and self-division are abrogated in the image Posthumus uses when the two at last embrace: "Hang there like fruit, my soul,/Till the tree die!" (263–4). It is an image which is impossible to dismantle: for we cannot tell whether his own soul or she herself is the anaphoric antecedent of "my soul," nor whether "there" is the space within his embracing arms or hers. Does he imagine Imogen hanging like fruit upon his fatherly support? Or does he imagine himself hanging upon her maternal support like a fruit which need never (till the tree die) be detached? This culminating moment annuls the dirge, offers fruit for the latter's dust. Yet it contains its own knowledge of finitude, despite its fantasy of merger and completion of self in other, for even the tree will, one day, die.

The soothsayer's culminating account, to Cymbeline, of his vision of peace is analogous in its mixing of gender. The eagle-Ceasar is indeterminately male and female, so therefore also is radiant Cymbeline in this mythological union of their powers:

> the Roman eagle,
> From south to west on wing soaring aloft,
> Lessen'd herself and in the beams o'th' sun
> So vanish'd; which foreshow'd our princely eagle,
> Th'imperial Caesar, should again unite
> His favor with the radiant Cymbeline,
> Which shines here in the west.   (470–6)

It is a strange, even monstrous valedictory emblem for a very strange play. Have we, with the aid of the psychoanalytic insights, made sense of it? Of any part of it? Has our attempt to "follow the path of the signifier," and to tell the other story of *Cymbeline* thrown light into the shadowy reaches of the textual unconscious which was our quarry?

The play has been inundated by fantasies of dispersed and reassembled families, parents, siblings, marriage partners; of split and recuperated identities; of "lopp'd branches, which, being dead many years, shall after revive, be jointed to the old stock, and freshly grow" (438–40). Implicit in all these has been an urgent will to transform the forces making for death and dissolution into a reaffirmation of procreative life. The *pater familias* of Act V, full of affection and happiness, joyful "mother to the birth of three" (369) is manifestly not the Cymbeline, the "*nom (non) du père*," of the beginning, as destructive in his tyrannical possessiveness as he was submissive to the wife who deceived and enthralled him, and as patently a projection of oedipal fantasy as was his poison-queen of an earlier infantile stage of development.

It is no doubt the sense of an unresolved strangeness that causes Murray Schwartz to judge the play "a failure" – "a play with a broken ego" (1976, 270), but this is because he focuses upon Posthumus as a case study in neurosis – Shakespeare's, and that of "the dominant ego of his age, polarised in its conception of sexual identity" (282) and its attitude to feminine power. "Shakespeare," he says, "has not yet found the psychic courage to admit that the fears and aggressions he evokes in *Cymbeline* reside in a father, and that their object is an unconsciously harbored mother imago" (283). This is absurd since either it postulates a Shakespeare who could only know what he knew by having undergone a course in the psychoanalytic theory of the Oedipus complex, or it does not remember that it was Shakespeare who wrote the play *Hamlet* some ten years before the composition of *Cymbeline*. Moreover, if it is a question of "psychic courage" in the probing of the inner life, I should think that *King Lear* alone should be sufficient evidence of Shakespeare's possession of that attribute. Not to mention *Coriolanus*.

Nevertheless we may still feel that there remains a gap in our perception of *Cymbeline*. The bits do not cohere. It stays fragmented in our minds, a bundle of lively, or lurid but disintegrated parts. The testing question with which this study began is whether we can close this gap, whether we can move through the Lacanian witticism from ellipse as textual gap to ellipse as transferential circuit in which text and reader can meet.

Fruitful in this respect is Charles Hofling's reminder that Shakespeare's mother died the year before *Cymbeline* is generally held to have been composed, and that in the same year a daughter was born to his own recently married favorite daughter. The following year Shakespeare returned to Stratford, and to his wife, after the twenty-year absence in London which followed the birth of his third child (1965, 133ff.). This is suggestive; and taken in tandem with the obsessively repetitive imagery of severance, fragmentation and recuperation precipitates a concluding insight.

Freud, in his reflections upon the Triple Goddess – the three significant women figures in a man's life – exhibits an odd amnesia. When he expands upon the story of the three caskets it is mother, wife and burying earth that he names, forgetting a fourth possibility.[9] Shakespeare's romances are, in effect, a riposte. The beloved, thaumaturgic daughters of these last plays supplement Freud's death-dominated triad. The three significant women in a man's life in these late plays are mother, wife and daughter, new life-bringer, who can reverse, at least in fantasy, the decline into death.

Consider the "death" of Fidele/Imogen. Belarious' "ingenious instrument" (IV.ii.186) is sounded for the first time since the death of the boys' supposed mother when Fidele dies, and she is to be buried beside the latter's grave. In her mock death she takes the place of Euriphile who took the place of the boys' real mother (who was also her own), whose place was taken by the deathly Queen mother. Lucius announces that no master had a page "so kind . . . so tender . . . so nurse-like" (V.v.86–8). She is not only herself symbolically reborn, she is the cause rebirth is in others, that is, in Cymbeline, the absent, occulted father, proxy for his author, the productions of whose imagination are all splinters of the self, of "His Majesty the Ego."[10] In this view the motivating, generating fantasy, or perplexity, of the play is located in the figure of the King, and it is this that enables us to move from Lacan's ellipse as a gap in the text, to the ellipse as a circuit connecting text and reader. If we unbind the text in this way, if we see Posthumus as a proxy for Cymbeline in the latter's absence, just as Iachimo and Cloten were proxies for Posthumus in his absence, and behind the whole series of figures a troubled author whose preoccupations the foregrounded stories screen, and while screening reveal, we can suddenly see the whole fable in a new light.

It is a father's deeply repressed desire for his daughter that is relayed through Posthumus, hence he is shackled and hampered in the conduct of his love. Hence the "killing" of Imogen, sham though it be, and the necrophilia of that nightmarish scene. Hence her rescue by a benign, protective father figure, whom she in turn "nurses," as Lucius makes a point of telling us. Yet in the recognition scenes there are still painful resonances: Imogen, it seems, deserts her "father" Lucius; Belarius reexperiences the loss of the children, "two of the sweet'st companions in the world" (V.v.349) that Cymbeline lost. The severing and reestablishing of parent/grown-child relationships is an arduous and troubled work of transformation, of the dislodging and redeployment of invested emotions, as we may learn from Shakespeare's dramas, if not from life. It is the work of late maturity, no benign retirement, but fraught with layer upon layer of old anxieties and hostilities, layer upon layer of new rivalries and jealousies. This is the work of the oneiric imagination throughout the late plays; and it is to this seedbed of Shakespeare's romances that *Cymbeline* can give us access.

4

Delusions and dreams:
The Winter's Tale

Death, as we all know, is not something to be looked at in the face.

(J.-B. Pontalis)

In *The Winter's Tale* the once mandatory dramatic "unities" – time, place, action and motivation tumble to the ground like a house of cards. Constructed out of two antithetical parts, in two different geographical locations, it is halved in the centre by a "wide gap of time" and propelled into action by an unmotivated outburst of ruinous rage. Among other notorious oddities, such as the bear-infested but nonexistent sea-coast of Bohemia, there is a memorable rogue who accompanies the second half of the play in a way which has defeated most attempts at interpretation.[1] These are no longer regarded as preposterous, as lapses, crudities or absurdities.[2] *The Winter's Tale* is safely ensconced among the masterpieces. Yet perplexities and uneasinesses remain.

Let me make a bold foray into the thicket of *The Winter's Tale*. If I were asked to formulate in one short sentence the gist of what *The Winter's Tale* is "about" I would say the following: In *The Winter's Tale* a child is lost, and a lost child is found: between these extremities *The Winter's Tale* runs its course. And I would add that the deeply embedded inner tale is Mamillius', a "sad tale" of "sprites and goblins" and of "a man" who "dwelt by a churchyard" (II.i.25–30), which has only a beginning, and is for Hermione's ear alone.

My attempt in the following pages is to reconstruct the fantasy which, I believe, animates and unifies the play, from which it derives its power to move us, and which determines and shapes its manifest drama. The fantasy has its roots in the deepest, most archaic, and most painful of our human experiences; yet, at the same time its expression by means of formal invention and mimetic verisimilitude, its orchestration of manifold means of dramatic representation and of dramatic utterance is particularly elaborate and rich. I believe that a rereading of *The Winter's Tale* receptive to the resonances of deep-level fantasy can take us beyond the traditional explanatory themes which are invoked as organizers and arbiters of meaning – the seasons of great creating nature, for instance, or the miracles of a benign providence – to uncover the sources of the play's emotional power. It can also take us beyond (or at least put into brackets) the orthodox psychoanalytic explications of Leonates' sudden onset of delusional jealousy.

In its own time the play was a masterpiece in a new and popular mode. The particular version of pastoral called *tragicomoedia* (or, as it was sometimes called, *comitragoedia*) had become over the two decades preceding the composition of *The Winter's Tale*, one of the central projects in the Renaissance literary itinerary. It had bred, among other taxonomic peculiarities, a Latin closet drama of 1612–14 by Mario Bettini subtitled *Hilarotragoedia Satyropastoralis* which, besides out-Heroding Polonius, offered a smorgasbord of situations, character types, figures, topoi, and devices from the Renaissance repertory. It also developed a legitimate hybrid genre called *commedia grave* which was a conjunction of features from Cinthio's *tragedia de lieto fin* and from Arcadian comedy.[3] Its declared intent was the mingling of hornpipes and funerals which Sidney had found so objectionable. Thus the compounding, conflating and juxtaposing of incompatible plots had become fashionable in late sixteenth-century Italy, intent upon a mannerist subversion of neoclassical rules, and an aesthetic of paradox and indeterminacy. That Shakespeare's art was affected by such trends is not in question. One recalls, among other anachronisms – English Whitsun pastoral rubbing shoulders with Greek oracles, for instance – the odd presence of Guilio Romano, Raphael's mannerist successor, at the court of Leontes, or at least within reach of Paulina's commission. As Rosalie Colie reminds us, "*The Winter's Tale* is an astonishingly *timely* play, seen against continental preoccupations" (1974, 265). That there is a craftsman's pride in the violence with which the two halves of the play are split apart, and the cunning with which they are spliced together, as if the controlling structures of tragedy and comedy were pitted against each other and locked in mortal combat, is perhaps indicated by the third gentleman's description of Paulina in the scene of reunions: "But O! the noble combat that 'twixt joy and sorrow was fought in Paulina! She had one eye declin'd for the loss of her husband, another elevated that the oracle was fulfill'd" (V.ii.72–6). *The Winter's Tale*, with its twinning of genres and generations, its gap (or compression) of time, its triumphantly double resolution and its bogus miracle is a contemporary *tour de force*. Pauline thus described, is a bizarre emblem of the play's duality, possibly a covert plea for the audience's admiration.

How are we to respond to this hybrid form? Are we merely to applaud a triumph of conscious virtuosity? We cannot easily say whether the tragedy is embedded in the comedy or vice versa. Is Leontes' destructive aberration a wintry episode in an ongoing unending story of growth and renewal? Or is the family good fortune a happy contingency in an ongoing unending Schopenhauerian story of loss and grief? Which of these *is* the *The Winter's Tale*? "A sad tale's best for winter" (II.i.25) Mamillius tells his mother and, since he is one of the play's two casualties, his view has a certain cogency; but does he point to part or whole? *The Winter's Tale*, fissured by its oppositions of time, place, tempo, mood, style, mode and genre is bound by innumerable linkages and mirrorings; yet in it tragedy will not absorb or synthesize comedy, nor comedy tragedy.

The gentleman who reports on the joyful reunion between

Leontes and Polixenes makes this very point, and is unable to read the signs: "There was speech in their dumbness, language in their very gesture; they look'd as they had heard of a world ransom'd, or one destroy'd" (V.ii.13–15).

The two halves of *The Winter's Tale* present us with a tragic structure powerfully compressed, and a recognizably familiar New Comedy in the pastoral mode which defers, but finally extends and deepens the anagnorisis. The final Act enacts a double resolution: the conflicts of both plots are defused by one and the same recognition – the discovery of the foundling Perdita – an admirable instance of the "well-tied knot" to which the writers of tragicomedy aspired, and a wish-fulfillment of the most tormenting of all human desires – to undo irreversible error.

The second part of the play, then, redeems the first, but it is also obsessively repetitive of the first, as if it were haunted by the same ghosts and goblins. New life is born in the first part and cast out to sea; new young love is born in the second, and cast out to sea, and in each case by "wintry" passions, Leontes' and Polixenes', doubles in their tyrannical ferocity as they were in their boyhood twinship. Antigonus saves an unacknowledged daughter from her father in the first part, Camillo an unrecognized son from his father in the second. The second part replays, reiterates the first in manifold ways. The triangle of the first part – Leontes, Hermione, Polixenes – is twice realigned, with intermingled variations, in the second: Leontes accuses his wife of relations with his old friend, and comes between them; or, if you will, the old friend comes between the couple. The old friend accuses his son of relations with Leontes' daughter, and comes between them; or, if you will, Hermione's daughter comes between father and son. Finally Leontes, momentarily tempted to come between his own daughter and the friend's son, sanctions their union. As James Edward Siemon puts it:

> Each of the two halves of the play has a wrathful king; innocent victims; a princess slandered; a servant who serves his master's highest interests by betraying him; a kingdom

without an heir or threatened with the loss of its heir; a voyage over a stormy sea; a providential revelation . . . each part has at its center two men and a woman: two "brothers" and a queen of Sicilia; father and son and a princess of Sicilia. There can be little doubt that the second part of the play represents a conscious variation on the themes and plot motives of the first. (1974, 13)

How do we respond to these obsessive doublings? The recurrences bind the contrasting structures, but they bind with a difference – as the suturing of a wound draws attention to the wound. They suggest the unstable asymmetry of a triad struggling, again and again, to right itself. The grip over our minds exerted by *The Winter's Tale* is beyond the cunning of connoisseurship or virtuosity. The play is not only a *tour de force* in contemporary dramaturgy; it is a *tour de force* in the theatre of reverie, which, the argument in these chapters maintains, is the mode of Shakespearean romance. There is therefore another kind of cunning which I would wish to invoke in an account of *The Winter's Tale*: that of the most cunning of interpreters, and of his subject matter.

In his "Revision of the Theory of Dreams," collected in *New Introductory Lectures*, Freud writes:

Franz Alexander (1925) has shown in a study on pairs of dreams that it not infrequently happens that two dreams in one night share the carrying-out of the dream's task by producing a wish-fulfilment in two stages if they are taken together, though each dream separately would not effect that result. Suppose, for instance, that the dream-wish had as its content some illicit action in regard to a particular person. Then in the first dream the person will appear undisguised, but the action will be only timidly hinted at. The second dream will behave differently. The action will be named without disguise, but the person will either be made unrecognizable or replaced by someone indifferent. This, you will admit, gives one an impression of actual cunning. Another and similar relation between the two members of a pair of dreams is found where one represents a punishment and the other the sinful wish-fulfilment. It amounts to this: "if one accepts the punishment for it, one can go on to allow oneself the forbidden thing." (1933, 56)

These remarks are extremely suggestive, though cast in terms too minatory and judgemental to be quite applicable to the eudaemonic ends of Shakespearean comedy. Freud's hypothetical case of a pair of dreams does not exactly fit the carriage of fantasy in Shakespeare's pair of interrelated plots, but his comment suggests a structural model with which to go to work. With *The Winter's Tale* in mind one would add a sentence to his: "Another and similar relation between two members of a pair of dreams is found where one represents a terror ineluctably realized and the other a restitutive wish-fulfillment." This, I shall argue, helps us to chart the trajectory of fantasy in *The Winter's Tale* and enables us to account for and respond to its particular force.

The text obtrudes its contradictory double nature from the very beginning. The prologue scene imparts preliminary information about the two kings' friendship, but the exchange of courtesies between Camillo and Archidamus is riddled by ambiguities – a palimpsest whose ulterior meanings subvert or nullify the decorous overt intention. "If you shall chance, Camillo, to visit Bohemia, on the like occasion whereon my services are now on foot, you shall see (as I have said) great difference betwixt our Bohemia and your Sicilia" (I.i.1–4); "We will give you sleepy drinks, that your senses (unintelligent of our insufficience) may, though they cannot praise us, as little accuse us" (13–16); "You pay a great deal too dear for what's given freely" (17–18); Sicilia and Bohemia "were train'd together in their childhoods; and there rooted betwixt them then such an affection, which cannot choose but branch now" (22–4). Benignly horticultural, the branch – metaphor for flourishing growth – is itself also a metaphor for parting and division; and the image, rebuslike, conceals (or does not conceal) the ubiquitous Elizabethan cuckold's horns. The euphuistic description of the two kings' friendship contains its own antithesis: "they have seem'd to be together, though absent; shook hands, as over a vast; and embrac'd as it were from the ends of oppos'd winds" (29–33). It is totally reversible, indeterminately an affirmation of their togetherness when apart, or their estrangement even when together. These double, or treble, entendres in which the two possibilities, the idyllic and the catastrophic, coexist reflect the larger structure of the play and of Leontes' dilemma. The rhetoric of courtesy slyly rehearses it seems, the entire ensuing drama.

In the grand opening scene too, Polixenes' "Nine changes of the wat'ry star" (I.ii.1) refers ostensibly to the duration of his absence from Bohemia. But the presence on stage of Leontes' pregnant queen ineluctably fills, so to speak, the semantic space, and magnetizes, or sexualizes, in consequence the entire subsequent text: "Without a burthen," "filled up," "standing in rich place," "what may chance/Or breed," "to tire your royalty" (to weary you? to wear your robes? to prey upon you?). If the unconscious is structured like a language, in Lacan's famous apothegm, this language certainly seems to be structured like an unconscious, in which the benign and the threatening are held in contradictory suspension. What are we to make of this unruly text which seems to be constructing its own counterplot in defiance of any narrative logic? For on the face of it, in the prologue the courtiers are merely exchanging prefatory courtesies. In Act I, scene ii Polixenes is politely refusing his friend's pressing hospitality. Equivocation in the dialogue with Leontes must surely undermine the speaker's own purpose, for Polixenes would be unlikely to be interested in insinuating into his host's mind suspicions of a liaison with the latter's wife, should there have been any such. Does Leontes hear what we hear? Does he hear what we are not supposed, as it were, to hear? Or are we privy to a communication neither of the protagonists hear?

William H. Matchett provides an ingenious answer:

> The language, no less than Hermione, is pregnant. Hermione, we are by now convinced, is accustomed to using more warmth with Polixenes. It is true that we must later discover that we were wrong, that this was all innocent, but

Shakespeare's dramatic method here is first to mislead *us* in order to hasten the process of misleading Leontes. He has in fact misled us twice; first in scene i by preparing us for innocent friendship and now in scene ii by presenting an image of guilt where there is in fact innocence. (1969, 96, and passim)

Matchett fails to explain, however, why it is the manifest meaning, the "innocent" meaning that is operative in the prologue scene whereas in scene ii he claims priority for the innuendo – the "guilty" meaning. By line 77 Polixenes' "Temptations have since been born to's," ostensibly an elegiac lament for the passing of childhood innocence, *we* hear, Matchett is persuaded, "a sophisticated understatement shared with Hermione and the audience behind Leontes' back" (97), and by this time "we would be wondering when Leontes will face what is going on." Similarly, Hermione's

> Th'offenses we have made you do we'll answer,
> If you first sinn'd with us   (I.ii.83–4)

is not, according to Matchett, to be read as a confidant disavowal but, with the accent upon "first," as a sly confession. Shakespeare's "masterful manipulation," in Matchett's reading, causes us to become suspicious long before Leontes does. We should feel, he says, not that Leontes is too rapidly jealous, but that he has been very slow about it. And the point? If we ourselves have been led to mistake innocence for guilt, how can we entirely blame Leontes?

M. Mahood, who preceded Matchett in the study of the ambiguities, disagrees:

> It is possible, of course, to read long-standing suspicion into all Leontes' speeches to Polixenes and Hermione, from the first appearance of the three characters. But this impairs the dramatic contrast between the happiness and harmony of the three characters when Polixenes has agreed to stay, and Leontes' subsequent outburst of passion ("Too hot, too hot"). . . . a sudden outburst of normally suppressed feelings,

which struggle for their release in savage wordplay." ((1957) 1971, 348)

However, she, intent upon evidence of a wise Shakespearean tolerance of inexplicable human frailty, does not explain why there should have been such an outburst. Both these astute Empsonians construe univocally, in terms of their differing interpretative purposes, the entire string of comments with which Leontes punctuates his wife's persuasion of Polixenes, although at any point in the series ("Tongue-tied, our Queen? (27), "Well said, Hermione" (33), "Is he won yet?" (86), and "At my request he would not./Hermione, my dearest, thou never spok'st/To better purpose" (87–9)) either a generous and gracious innocence or a dissimulated but tormenting suspicion might be what is signified.

Let us attempt to relocate Leontes within the linguistic web of this scene. The undertones in Polixenes' "nine changes" speech cannot, with any dramatic feasibility, incriminate Polixenes, but they can be heard by Leontes with certain triggering effects. The mere reference to the number nine, Freud noted, "whatever its connection, directs our attention to the phantasy of pregnancy" ("A Seventeenth Century Demon-ological Neurosis" (1923) SE.XIX,93). This is a useful reminder, for if we read the resonances of the "nine months" speech as pointing towards Leontes' fantasy rather than as incriminating Polixenes, we then are enabled to perceive that a certain anxiety attends the fact, in itself, of his wife's condition. Polixenes has left his throne without a burden, he says. For Leontes "burden" may well evoke the thought of that with which his own throne is "filled up." In the ambivalence of "to tire your royalty," the hint of succession is subverted by the simultaneous hint of usurpation. If Leontes is reading himself in Polixenes' text, then "like a cipher standing in rich place" (I.ii.6–7) succinctly suggests the nothingness, the emptiness of exclusion from a once experienced plenitude. Our third ear, moreover, catches a disturbing note in both Hermione's exchanges with her husband. It is not perhaps Hermione's most felicitious move to offer to allow Leontes to overstay as long as a whole month in Bohemia should the occasion arise, and with the assurance: "yet, good deed, Leontes,/I love thee not a jar o'th'clock behind/What lady she her lord" (42–4). Any lady? Whatever lady you care to mention? It is an oddly noncommittal claim, surely, but worse is to follow:

> What? have I twice said well? When was't before? . . .
> But once before I spoke to th'purpose? when?
> Nay, let me hav't; I long.   (89–101)

This is spoken jestingly, of course, but it is not unknown for jests to be used to camouflage resentments. Neither Leontes' description of the "three crabbed months" which soured themselves to death before Hermione's "I am yours forever" was uttered, nor his pointed reference to his dagger, muzzled "Lest it should bite its master, and so prove,/[As ornament] oft does, too dangerous" (157–8) do much to mitigate the impression we might receive of a couple in considerable marital stress, if not positive crisis.

It is in this context that Polixenes describes a nostalgic fantasy of perfect unity, when he and Leontes were as "twinn'd lambs, that did frisk i'th'sun,/And bleat the one at th'other" exchanging "innocence for innocence" (67–9).[4] The yearning is for the timeless – "Two lads that thought . . . to be boy eternal" (63–65) – and, significantly, the speechless: for a moment, known in infancy and long since lost, of undifferentiated oneness with another being. Hermione, jesting, provokes the insertion into the scene of the mutations, the depradations, of time – "By this we gather/You have tripp'd since" (75–6). Polixenes' reply is fervent:

>   O my most sacred lady,
> Temptations have since then been born to's: for
> In those unfledg'd days was my wife a girl;
> Your precious self had then not cross'd the eyes
> Of my young playfellow   (76–9)

hers is flippant:

>   Grace to boot!
> Of this make no conclusion, lest you say
> Your queen and I are devils. Yet go on,
> Th'offenses we have made you do we'll answer,
> If you first sinn'd with us.   (80–4)

and Leontes' entire string of comments, as we have seen, is opaquely ambiguous until his explicit. "Too hot, too hot!" (108):

> I have *tremor cordis* on me; my heart dances,
> But not for joy; not joy. This entertainment
> May a free face put on, derive a liberty
> From heartiness, from bounty, fertile bosom,
> And well become the agent; 't may, I grant.
> But to be paddling palms and pinching fingers,
> As now they are, and making practic'd smiles
> As in a looking glass; and then to sigh, as 'twere
> The mort o'th'deer – O, that is entertainment
> My bosom likes not, nor my brows. Mamillius,
> Art thou my boy? . . .
>   How now, you wanton calf,
> Art thou my calf?   (110–20, 126)

Leontes' torment is felt and uttered first as a problem of doubt, of what he can know, be sure of, in respect of his wife's fidelity, and subsequently as conviction of her sexual betrayal, but the question of adultery, we are enabled to perceive, is a mask, or a defence against a breach in his certainty which lies far deeper, in infantile fears of isolation, separation and abandonment. Leontes has been (visibly) separated, isolated, by the *tête-à-tête* between Hermione and Polixenes, especially by the intimacies of the twinned lambs exchange; but he has already been separated or isolated by Hermione's new intimacy with her unborn child. That it is by the archaic rage of a sibling rivalry for an undivided mother that he is overthrown is perhaps confirmed later by the ferocious violence with which he would consign the babe (and its mother) to the flames, in

Act II, scene iii, would see it "commit[ted] to the fire" (96); "I'll ha'thee burned" (114); "Better burn it now" (156).

It is the ancient loss, I believe the play tells us, that lies at the root of Leontes' seizure. There is, we are told, in every delusion a grain of truth. Hermione does betray Leontes, with her children, and it is the repetition of that maternal betrayal which is displaced upon the supposed adulterers, doubly determined figures in the primal drama. If we take a cue from psychoanalytic theory it is in such primal drama that all tragedy is rooted, and from its unassuaged pain that theatre-going draws its appeal. Leontes himself sets up the structure of a fantasied primal scene, in which he is the excluded third, spying, watching, testing, angling – "I am angling now,/ Though you perceive me not how I give line. . . . How she holds up the neb, the bill to him!" (I.ii.180–3) – trapping Hermione in a double bind: "How thou lov'st us, show in our brother's welcome" (174). If she is cold she will appear an uncompliant and disobedient wife; if warm, a self-betraying adulteress; she cannot win, nor does he wish her to win, for beneath the available postures of patriarchal male jealousy ("Should all despair/That have revolted wives, the tenth of mankind/ Would hang themselves" (188–200) and "Go play, boy, play. Thy mother plays, and I/Play too, but so disgrac'd a part, whose issue/Will hiss me to my grave; contempt and clamor/Will be my knell" (187–9)) lies the threat that is the greater because it is unknown. "Gone already" (185) on the face of it refers to the speed with which Hermione and Polixenes vanish together into the garden, but its resonance surely comes from an absence long ago experienced.

Ostensibly Leontes' questioning of Mamillius' likeness to himself expresses a worry about his paternity of the boy, but if this were really so, surely the answer would not be so insistently affirmative. What does he seek as he gazes into the face of his son, his "sweet villain," flesh of his flesh? It is a "copy" of his own – they are "almost as like as eggs" (note the image of symbiotic enclosure and totality) though it is false women who say so (122–36, passim). It is the paternity, after all, of the second child, not of Mamillius, that has been, if it has, placed in doubt. It is that imminent interloper who has reawakened the archaic loss, the archaic grief and rage, has made Leontes, at this moment, a replaced, or supplanted child, reliving the anguish of the mother's betrayal.

Dissimulating his agitation Leontes avows the "folly" of his "tenderness" for Mamillius:

> Looking on the lines
> Of my boy's face, methoughts I did recoil
> Twenty-three years, and saw myself unbreech'd,
> In my green velvet coat . . .
> How like (methought) I then was to this kernel,
> This squash, this gentleman. Mine honest friend,
> Will you take eggs for money?   (153–61)

We recall "We are almost as like as eggs" a few moments before, so that it is possible to interpret the question as a pained recognition of the illusoriness (as against the reality of money) of the unity-in-identity, the existential certainty that he had longed to find, if not in the mother, then at least in the mirror of his son's "welkin eye" (136). Then he turns to Polixenes with a question for his "brother": "Are you so fond of your young prince as we/Do seem to be of ours?" (163–4); and receives the expected tenderly affectionate reply:

> If at home, sir,
> He's all my exercise, my mirth, my matter;
> Now my sworn friend, and then mine enemy;
> My parasite, my soldier, statesman, all.
> He makes a July's day short as December,
> And with his varying childness, cures in me
> Thoughts that would thick my blood.   (165–71)

It is worth pausing a moment over that reply. Why would one wish a long summer day to be as short as a winter one? On the face of it Polixenes is describing childish games – he is a father who enjoys playing cowboys and Indians or cops and robbers with his young son – but can we ignore the subversive connotations of "enemy," of "parasite," above all of the strange inversion of July and December? The game itself acts out subliminal hostilities. Thoughts that would thick the blood are indeed soothed, stilled, by the charm of a child but the child is also a threat, a supplanter, a usurper. The face that is his own will one day efface his own. Leontes hears what we hear and replies, "So stands this squire officed with me" (172–3). The strange double message of Polixenes reflects, then, an emotion shared by these two twinned figures, and enables us to take a further step in the understanding of Leontes.

Leontes' passionate cleaving to the boy is rooted in identification – they are both ousted rivals for the mother's love – but it is also traversed by the deeper, unrecognized source of dread. He sees himself in Mamillius: the child in himself, his double (154–5), but he also sees his successor, and his death. Later, we recall, he cannot bear Paulina's insistence upon the new-born baby's resemblance to himself.

It becomes of the greatest interest to follow the course of Leontes' struggle against the upsurge of a turbulence which threatens to overthrow him, his half-aware struggle to maintain a foothold in reality:

> Come, sir page . . .
> Most dear'st, my collop! Can thy dam? – may't be?
> Affection! thy intention stabs the centre.
> Thou dost make possible things not so held
> Communicat'st with dreams (how can this be?),
> With what's unreal thou co-active art,
> And fellow'st nothing. Then 'tis very credent
> Thou mayst co-join with something, and thou dost
> (And that beyond commission), and I find it
> (And that to the infection of my brains
> And hard'ning of my brows).   (135–46)

This speech has been much commented upon. I think we can best understand it as exhibiting the moment of the switch-over in Leontes' thinking from the rational procedures of reality testing to the autistic, associational imagery of the primary processes, the imagery produced by the self's inner needs and dreads.[5] It is his last bulwark. Henceforth ratiocination itself will be flooded by fantasy, saturated by an influx of representations welling up from the depths of the mind, eluding all attempts at repression. If "affection" is glossed, as it often is, to refer to Hermione's alleged aberrant passion, which stabs to the very center of Leontes' (or the world's) being, the rest of the speech becomes extremely obscure;[6] but suppose we read it as a rearguard action, so to speak, half in sight, half in blindness, of a mind on the very brink of a self-induced, defensive delusion? "Affection" then is his own jealousy, which, seeking confirmation in reality has found, "communicat[ing] with dreams . . . with what's unreal," only that which feeds its flames. What if these intuitions do indeed stab the center, the bull's eye? The acknowledged power of fantasy to find a bush a bear now presents itself as doubly forceful confirmation of its divinatory powers when the bush really is a bear! Caught in these toils this Shakespearean snowman experiences the

> intricate evasions of as,
> In things seen and unseen, created from nothingness . . .
> The heavens, the hells, the worlds, the longed for lands[7]

and totally embraces the fiction which protects him, with the possessive masculine postures available to him in his society, from the deeper vulnerability, the unrecognized source of dread. Hence, in the flood of obscene images which follows, birth and copulation, entry and exit are scarcely to be distinguished.

>   Gone already!
> Inch-thick, knee-deep, o'er head and ears a forked one! . . .
> And many a man there is (even at this present,
> Now, while I speak this) holds his wife by th'arm,
> That little thinks she has been sluic'd in's absence,
> And his pond fish'd by his next neighbor – by
> Sir Smile, his neighbor. Nay, there's comfort in't,
> Whiles other men have gates, and those gates open'd,
> As mine, against their will. . . .
>   Be it concluded,
> No barricado for a belly. Know't,

It will let in and out the enemy,
With bag and baggage.   (I.ii.185–206, passim)

Earlier, in the exchange with Mamillius on the need to be
"neat" the threat of the primary process image-language of
dream is still under control, though the pressure of its
metaphors to subsume reality is formidably great:

>   Come, captain,
> We must be neat; not neat, but cleanly, captain:
> And yet the steer, the heifer, and the calf
> Are all call'd neat. – Still virginalling
> Upon his palm? How now, you wanton calf,
> Art thou my calf? . . .
> Thou want'st a rough pash and the shoots that I have
> To be full like me   (122–9)

Now his world is a bestiary: "How she holds up the neb! the
bill to him!" (183). Now Leontes is entirely at the mercy of his
fantasy, as if the whole lexis is alive with pointing fingers, or
with poisoned arrows. Every word of Camillo in the dialogue
between them at once inflames his imagination and provides
proof positive for his conviction: "You had much ado to make
his anchor hold/When you cast out it still came home"
(213–14); "Satisfy/Th'entreaties of your mistress? *Satisfy*?/Let
that suffice" (233–5; my italics). Hermione is a "hobbyhorse
. . . rank as any flax-wench" (276–7); were her liver as infected
as her life, "she would not live/The running of one glass"
(304–6). In his persuasion of Camillo fantasy positively parades
itself, ostentatiously, as reality-testing, but reality is no longer
separable from image:

>   Is whispering nothing?
> Is leaning cheek to cheek? is meeting noses?
> Kissing with inside lip? stopping the career
> Of laughter with a sigh . . .
>   horsing foot on foot?
> Skulking in corners? wishing clocks more swift?
> Hours, minutes? noon, midnight? and all eyes
> Blind with the pin and web but theirs . . .

                    Is this nothing?
Why then the world and all that's in't is nothing,
The covering sky is nothing, Bohemia nothing,
My wife is nothing, nor nothing have these nothings,
If this be nothing.   (284–95)[8]

Rhetorically, the figure he employs is an apodiosis, the indignant rejection of an argument as impertinent or absurdly false (Lanham, 1968, 13), but the ratiocinative appeal to items of evidence virtually conjures an act of intercourse into being. The body imagery, progressing from cheeks, noses, inside lip, horsing foot on foot, to the metaphorically sexual pin and web, and the "covering" sky, exacerbates an inflamed imagination, verbally creates the coupling that he imagines watching, that we imagine watching with him.

This "everything" with which Leontes now fills his dread-fully experienced nothingness (we recall "a cipher standing in rich place" (6–7)) denudes and impoverishes him, diminishes his very being – he is a "pinch'd thing" (51) – while it fills him with a sexual revulsion which the rhetoric of rational argu-mentation, again, to Camillo, ignites, rather than defuses. The metaphor of a soiled name collapses into the literality of a soiled bed, repulsive, loathsome:

Dost think I am so muddy, so unsettled,
To appoint myself in this vexation, sully
The purity and whiteness of my sheets
(Which to preserve is sleep, which being spotted
Is goads, thorns, nettles, tails of wasps)   (325–30)

Antigonus, whose rhetoric of denial echoes and aggravates his master's – if Hermione is "honor-flawed" he will "geld" his daughters (II.i.145, 147) – is rebuked for lacking just such enflamed – enlightened! – "seeing" as "communicat'st with dreams, with what's unreal": "You smell this business with a sense as cold/As is a dead man's nose; but I do see't, and feel't" (151–2). Leontes has seen the spider in the cup, and "cracks his gorge, his sides,/With violent hefts" (44–5), vomiting what he drinks.

What the play has exhibited is the process of self-entrapment whereby a deeply confused, insecure and unhappy man enmeshes himself in the web that he spins to defend himself from thoughts that lie too deep for knowledge. The force and vividness with which primary process imagery invades the mind and speech of Leontes make him an astonishingly realistic, individualized figure. We can be lured into reacting to "him" as not merely realistic, but virtually real. Yet he is a fabrication, an epiphenomenon of the text. "What does Leontes want?" we ask, inducting ourselves into an invented mind as we simultaneously watch the manner of its invention. "What does Leontes want?" is thus, strictly speaking, a rhetorical question. What Leontes, or any textual personage wants is what we ourselves could conceivably want were our world constructed out of the same set of displaced signifiers. What Leontes wants is what we discover to be comfortable, as we adjust empathetic introspection to the text's evocations, its figures, its twists and turns, its insistences, its peculiarities, with a meaningful scheme of things. Clues to that meaningful scheme of things we find wherever we can – in the language that we share with the Shakespearean personae, in the language that we no longer share with the Shakespearean personae, but that has to be reexplicated, in the language of symbols which is a remarkably tenacious subdivision of the shared language.

Spider venom, folklore informs us, is effective only if seen when the cup is drained. Leontes' metaphor for the curse of knowledge comes from this source. Spiders, psychoanalytic lore informs us, unconsciously symbolize devouring mother imagos;[9] but in whose unconscious? Leontes'? Shakespeare's? The reader's? The fact that just that metaphor occurs at this point is surely interesting, and I offer it as a test case for the usefulness of the portmanteau notion of a textual unconscious, which, in terms of the Lacanian ellipse, includes the circuit from author to reader via the fictional persona who is no more than a synechdoche – a part standing for the whole of the textual transaction.

Our understanding of the fixation which will give Leontes

no peace until it has compelled him to its own recognition is further advanced in the next phase of the play. Act II opens with Hermione, nearing her time and understandably bothered by her lively young son. "Take the boy to you; he so troubles me, Tis past enduring," she says (II.i.1). Her ladies, and the precocious Mamillius, who, we note, doesn't want to be treated "as if I were a baby still" (5), amuse themselves happily enough with reciprocal teasing, but there has been a rejection; and whatever wounded feelings we may impute to Mamillius can hardly be said to be mollified by the first lady's deliberate provocation "we shall/Present our services to a fine new prince/One of these days," says the First Lady, "and then you'll wanton with us, If we would have you" (16–19). The episode ends with renewed intimacy, out of earshot of the "cricket" ladies, between Mamillius and his mother, now recovered. A momentary maternal rejection, a provocation to sibling jealousy, a child's game effort to master fear with a story – this utterly ordinary little nursery scene has effectively reminded us of the griefs and losses that haunt the minds of children like the very sprites and goblins in Mamillius' tale; and it throws a melancholy light upon Leontes' breakdown.

What Leontes sees is the intimate communion of mother and son, Hermione and the boy with the mother-like name, from which he in his isolation is excluded, as he believed he was at the beginning, as Mamillius has just been. There is certainly no sport in his savage "Give me the boy. I am glad you did not nurse him ... Away with him! and let her sport herself/With that she's big with" (56–9, passim). Leontes is now a man driven by an unassuagable rage, defended only by the revengeful jealousy to which he clings, which he will not relinquish and from which he will not emerge until he has cast out his new-born infant to well-nigh certain destruction, received the news of Mamillius' death and, in effect, hounded Hermione to hers.

It is the news of Mamillius' death that brings him to his senses, releases him from the grip of the fantasy which the sexual jealousy masks. The key to that deepest level fantasy is to be found in Leontes' reiterated "nothing" in the speech quoted above. What the speech contends is that the evidence of Hermione's infidelity is so palpable as to be impossible to ignore. Its rhetorical form is the setting out of an impossible postulate: if whispering, etc. is nothing, then nothing is anything; but the ulterior meaning of these frenetically iterated "nothings" is best understood as a rhetorical barricade against the admission of that which "has already been experienced" – I take the phrase from D.W. Winnicott's account of the "fear of breakdown" (1974, 104). "There are moments," he writes, "when a patient needs to be told that the breakdown, a fear of which destroys his or her life, *has always already been*." It is something the ego is unable to encompass because it is unthinkable: "a fear of the original agony which caused the defence . . . a fact that is carried round hidden away in the unconscious." Leontes' sense of nothingness, of emptiness, of annihilation is exactly that state which "cannot be remembered except by being experienced for the first time now." What we cannot remember we are forced to repeat, as we know. The death of the child who is Leontes', who is Leontes, following the abandonment of the other child that he feared, is thus the terror, the unthinkable agony, which is experienced "for the first time now."

Winnicott's insight illuminates to perfection the plight of Leontes, the backward drift which the tragic part of *The Winter's Tale* articulates. The nightmare of the child's death realizes the terror of a child's death which has already been, which has always already been, for Leontes as for Everyman. It is because that dread resonates with our own most primal terrors that we yield with such pleasure to the counterfantasy of the pastoral in Act IV, the transition to which, however, must first engage our attention.

The central scene of Act III, and of the play, is the great scene of the trial in which Leontes arraigns his Queen in a travesty of the justice he invokes. The scene shows Leontes totally isolated, and imprisoned, in his wounded narcissism. She is dignified, noble, abused as wife, as mother, as daughter ("The Emperor of Russia was my father. O, that he were alive, and here beholding/His daughter's trial" (III.ii.119–20)) by this unleashed male aggression. He is omnipotent, punitive, persecutory; she defenceless, deprived of her children, dragged from her prison childbed. "Sir," she says,

> You speak a language that I understand not.
> My life stands in the level of your dreams,
> Which I'll lay down.   (80–2)

One of the remarkable features of *The Winter's Tale* is the degree of unaware awareness with which its characters are endowed. We have already heard Leontes struggling, half-knowingly, with his own conflicting modes of cognition. Now his scathingly scornful reply, ironically affirming what it denies, causes one to shudder at the identity of rhetorical denial with its unconscious counterpart:

> Your actions are my dreams.
> You had a bastard by Polixenes,
> And I but dreamt it.   (82–4)

In terms of formal tragedy the scene enacts both reversal and recognition. Its action is the inevitable issue of choices already made –the culmination of error – and results in the ironically irreversible fatality which marks the midpoints of Shakespeare's tragic structures. Hermione, blameless, is condemned, but the oracle justifies her. The oracle is read but its message defied. Mamillius' death – immediate nemesis – is announced, Hermione collapses and to the now heartstruck Leontes is brought the news of her death. Leontes is led away to his sorrows, but we do not witness his terrible remorse. The play, as we know, will swerve away from tragic closure into the luxury of a dream of undoing, but the passage from nightmare to dream is mediated by another death.

Since *Measure for Measure* Shakespeare has bettered his instruction in the art of tragi-comic conjunction. In *Measure for Measure* the genre shift occurs abruptly, at the height of the crisis of Act III, with an unprecedented change of style, diction and mode. In *The Winter's Tale*, Act III, the Act which at once opens the breach between its two localities and bridges them, *obtrudes* its intermediary function, achieving a remarkable chiastic interlocking, both formal and symbolic. Act III consists of three scenes symmetrically divided to form a triptych. The two flanking scenes suggest the two antagonistic drives which tragicomedy commingles, each representing a landscape of the mind appropriate to the two opposed halves of the play. For Cleomenes and Dion on their way back from the oracle the climate is "delicate, the air most sweet,/Fertile the isle" (III.i.1–2); the sacrifice was "ceremonious, solemn, and unearthly" (7), their journey "rare, pleasant, speedy" (14). This scenic symbolism suggests the landscape of a mind whole and at peace. In extreme contrast with the benign and sensuous serenity of this *locus amoenus*, a maternal body, is the "savage clamor" (III.iii.56) of the Bohemian coast where Antigonus lands with his charge. Scene iii recounts the fate of the "poor souls" aboard Antigonus' ship, and of Antigonus himself, against a seascape ruinous, disintegrated and chaotic: "I am not to say it is a sea, for it is now the sky; betwixt the firmament and it you cannot thrust a bodkin's point. . . . how it chafes, how it rages . . . now the ship boring the moon with her mainmast, and anon swallow'd with yeast and froth, as you'd thrust a cork into a hogshead. And then for the land-service, to see how the bear tore out his shoulder bone, how he cried to me for help . . . how the sea flap-dragon'd it . . . how the poor souls roar'd, and the sea mock'd them; and how the poor gentleman roar'd, and the bear mock'd him, both roaring louder than the sea or weather. . . . I have not wink'd since I saw these sights. The men are not yet cold under water, nor the bear half din'd on the gentleman" (87–106, passim). The clown's imagery grotesquely mingles pity and terror, records dismemberment with a cannibalistic detachment, condenses orgasm and death-throe. Where the temperate climate of Cleomenes evokes a longed-for restitution still to come, this chaotic seascape figures the breakdown already undergone.

The ambassadors to the oracle in scene i, certain of Hermione's innocence, anticipated rescue and remedy, yet catastrophe occurred; the Bohemian shepherd who rescues the abandoned babe has no doubt about ill-doing: "Though I am not bookish, yet I can read waiting-gentlewoman in the scape. This has been some stair-work, some trunk-work, some behind-door-work," he says (72, 73), yet he is the agent of deliverance. The babe is rescued and the treasure found, to the haunting rhythm of the shepherd's "thou met'st with things dying, I with things new-born" (113–14), as the play moves into its remedial phase, accompanied by the pitiful and pitying figure of Hermione in Antigonus' strange vision.

Antigonus' gruesome death and his vision have puzzled many commentators. "Shakespeare's solution," says Tillyard, referring to the problem of transition from the tragic to the pastoral, "is to drive the tortured world of Leontes and Hermione to a ridiculous extreme in Antigonus' vision. In so doing he really puts an end to it" ((1938), in Kermode (1938, 78)). There is nothing ridiculous, I submit, in Antigonus' powerful soliloquy as he deposits the babe on the Bohemian shore. It is a premonition of his own death – he will never see his wife again – and the account of an hallucination. It records an experience truly uncanny:

> I have heard (but not believed) the spirits o'th'dead
> May walk again. If such thing be, thy mother
> Appear'd to me last night; for ne'er was dream
> So like a waking. To me comes a creature,
> Sometimes her head on one side, some another –
> I never saw a vessel of like sorrow,
> So fill'd, and so becoming   (III.iii.16–22)

Antigonus himself is in doubt about the status of his vision, uncertain whether he has dreamed a dream or seen a ghost. He settles, with somewhat anachronist Protestant scepticism, for the ghost theory – "for this once, yea superstitiously" (40) – he believes that "this was so, and no slumber" (39). We may recognize hallucination (for which there was as yet no word available in Shakespeare's vocabulary)[10] but what, we must ask, is its function in the drama.

In accordance with the principles of splitting and replication in dramatic (and dream) representation when psychic burdens become too heavy to be borne, Antigonus, I suggest, is a part of the Leontes persona. Counterpart to Paulina, who is an externalized conscience to Leontes throughout, he is the latter's destructive, ambivalent will in the abandonment of the babe. He has already echoed Leontes' violent, reflex misogyny (he would "geld" his daughters should Hermione prove false, we recall). The oscillation in his view of women as either ideal or animal represents the ferocious need of the frail masculine ego for a feminine ideal which will defend it against Oedipal anxieties. He has born the brunt of Leontes' projective accusation regarding his emasculated dependency upon his "Dame Partlet." The apparition he experiences is an angelic suffering figure, who was nevertheless, he is persuaded, guilty, and therefore justly punished. Leontes' secret sharer, he thus reflects the violent psychic split which was his master's; and suffers his retributory death as scapegoat for the latter's guilt. If his vision represents, in already fading retrospect, the precedent split in Leontes, Antigonus' behavior prefigures the reparative renewal of tenderness, of compassion – "Blossom, speed thee well" (III.iii.46) which will take the place of the flaying self-punishment Leontes embraces at the end of the trial scene. A similar transition is adumbrated by Paulina when, following her

> O thou tyrant . . .
> A thousand knees,
> Ten thousand years together, naked, fasting,
> Upon a barren mountain, and still winter
> In storm perpetual, could not move the gods
> To look that way thou wert   (III.ii.207–14)

she is moved to pity him.

In both the tragic Shakespearean form and the comic, the penultimate Act plays with remedy. In tragedy possible remedies (like the return of Cordelia in *Lear*) are, so to speak, offered, only to be snatched away, terribly, by the onward momentum of the consequences of previous fatal errors. In comedy remedy, the absent identity, or person, or information required to solve the errors and conflicts which in the play's center come to an impasse is found, or begins to be found. In

The Winter's Tale this is indeed the case, except that disaster, for Leontes, has already happened, and that this "remedy," the finding and eventual recovery of Perdita, is given an entire expanded, separate comic plot of its own, which, however, reproduces, as it were, compulsively, the plot which fathers it.

The play's structure of duplications allows for complex reevaluations, as samenesses and differences are simultaneously taken in. As has been pointed out, the second part reiterates the first. It repeats the story of rupturing, envious jealousy, of fear of usurpation, with Polixenes doubling for Leontes, Florizel for his father Polixenes, and Perdita for her mother Hermione. Polixenes' disavowal of his previous approval of the marriage of "a gentler scion to the wildest stock" (IV.iv.93) when his own posterity is at issue is as violent as the flare-up in Leontes of a possessive and dispossessed rage. Polixenes' ferocity is partly conventional – expected in a New Comedy *senex* – as is Florizel's unfilial indifference: "One being dead," he says, "I shall have more than you can dream of yet" (387–8); and in reply to the question whether he has a father, and whether his father knows of his betrothal, his cavalier reply is: "I have; but what of him? . . . He neither does, nor shall" (392–3). Partly, at least, the generational conflict serves as a recurrence and confirmation of the usurpation theme in the first part of the play.

Yet, as indeed the play informed us in its first lines: "If you shall chance, Camillo, to visit Bohemia, on the like occasion whereon my services are now on foot, you shall see (as I have said) great difference betwixt our Bohemia and your Sicilia" (I.i.1–4). *The Winter's Tale* realizes its dream of a second chance in Bohemia, through its second generation, as well as its second genre. New life means new possibilities, new comprehensions, new solutions. In Bohemia, the generational conflict is acted out overtly, in its own terms and without dissimulation. The desires of the young lovers in Bohemia are not undermined by the grip of archaic fears, by the drift back into the claustral recesses of the mind: "I was not much afeard," says Perdita, despite the dire threats of Polixenes,

> for once or twice
> I was about to speak, and tell him plainly
> The self-same sun that shines upon his court
> Hides not his visage from our cottage, but
> Looks on alike.   (IV.iv.443–6)

And Florizel is "but sorry, not afeard" (463) as he renounces "succession" to be "heir to [his] affection" (480–1).

The green world in *The Winter's Tale* is a return, not of an unreconstructed childhood but to a childhood – a fantasied (benign) childhood, where fathers are good shepherds, and children unthreatened, and therefore unafraid – restitutive, rather than exorcist in its emotional effect. The sprites and goblins of Mamillius' sad tale have been exorcized, violently, in the first part of the play. In the wide gap of time, off stage, expiation is undergone by the absent Leontes, mourning his losses. What the play's dreaming tells us is that expiation, self-condemnation, is not enough. If consciousness is not irradiated by a knowledge of what could constitute a transcendence both of isolation and of fusion, a harmony of needs, mutual recognition, freely expressed desire, no reparation, or rehabilitation, or renewal will take place. It is this possibility of a different outcome that the pastoral fantasy of Florizel and Perdita, most eudaemonic of Shakespeare's green worlds, opens up. Nobody, perhaps, puts it better than the shepherd:

> He says he loves my daughter.
> I think so too; for never gaz'd the moon
> Upon the water as he'll stand and read
> As 'twere my daughter's eyes.   (171–4)

What Perdita says with flowers undoes courtly duplicity without foregoing courtesy, as she tactfully adjusts her floral offerings to her guests, or rather to the age her guests would like to think they belong to, while nevertheless stubbornly maintaining her position regarding gillyvors. The flowers mesh into a Renaissance debate about art and nature (read: culture and heredity) which is relevant to the question of a Queen of curds and cream, but they are richly symbolic in other ways too. They mediate the passage from winter to spring by themselves moving, so to speak, backwards through the seasons: Perdita begins with the offering of rosemary and rue which last through the winter, attempts to mollify Polixenes' response to the gift of wintry flowers with an emphasis on the present autumn season, "not yet on summer's death, nor on the birth/Of trembling winter" (80–1), negotiates the gillyvors hurdle triumphantly with the lavender, mint, savory, marjoram and marigold "of middle summer" (107) and only then turns to Florizel with the famous lyrical invocation of the flowers of the spring, and of Persephone. Perdita's mythopoeia conjugates erotic awakening with seasonal rebirth, moving from the virgin branches, Proserpina's fallen flowers, the daffodils that take the winds of March with beauty, the dim, sweet eyelids of Juno, Cytherea's breath, the pathos of primroses "that die unmarried ere they can behold/Bright Phoebus in his strength," to the frankly phallic "bold oxslips" and "crown imperial" (118–26) and the final routing of Thanatos:

No, like a bank for Love to lie and play on;
Not like a corse; or if, not to be buried,
But quick and in my arms.   (130–2)

The separate Perdita story is a chapter in the Greek romance narrative of long-lost children, family vicissitudes and family reunions, but it is also a recognizable Terentian comedy with all the formulaic constituents: a foundling, a casket to provide identification when required, a high-born lover in disguise on account of parental disapproval, the fortunate disclosure not only of a desirable identity for the girl, but positively of her own lost parents, and the restoration of amity both within and between the families concerned. It even has a tricky servant to negotiate the errors, mishaps, and mistaken identities of the comic plot in which young lovers outwit or evade parental disapproval. But has it?

Autolycus has been Florizel's servant, we learn, but is no longer, though we are not told why he is "out of service" (IV.iii.14). He is now in business on his own but nevertheless it is he who exchanges clothes with Florizel so that his may provide the prince with a further disguise for his escape with Perdita from the wrath of Polixenes. Later, removing another piece of disguise, his peddlar's beard, for the purpose, he becomes ambassador from Perdita's shepherd father to Polixenes to whom the bundle is to be shown, thus proving the shepherd adoptive father only and so saving him from retribution for his adopted daughter's fatal charms. This is a con, however, and instead of conducting the shepherd-with-bundle to Polixenes' court, he conducts him to his former master's escape ship, wondering, reprobate that he is, how it is that Fortune insists upon tempting him into "honesty" do what he will. (IV.iv.831). These machinations of Autolycus in fact delay the discovery of the bundle's contents, so that the secret remains undiscovered until the shepherd carries his fardel to Polixenes himself (now also in Sicilia), and is catapulted into the status of "gentleman born" (V.ii.127) as a reward. It turns out, therefore, that Autolycus, who prides himself upon the possession of an open ear, a quick eye, a nimble hand and a good rogue's nose for the smelling out of opportunities for advancement has allowed himself to be deprived of an obvious bonus. Ebullient as ever, he resigns himself to the set-back: "But 'tis all one to me; for had I been the finder-out of this secret, it would not have relish'd among my other discredits" (V.ii.121). In the role of tricky servant, it seems, Autolycus does not shine, but he has other resources for making a living, learned partly from the distinguished company of sharp-witted vagabonds who were beginning to populate the literature of the picaresque, and partly from his Ovidian genealogy. Ovidian Autolycus (in Golding's translation "a wyly pye" without peer for filching and theft) was, it will be recalled, the son of no other than Mercury/Hermes.

Hermes, hardly out of his cradle, was already stealing the oxen of Apollo, who was appeased however, by the child's skill at the lyre (which he invented by stretching strings across a tortoise shell). Messenger, herald, conductor of souls between the worlds of the living and the dead, protector of travelers, whose signposts and landmarks were named for him, worship-

ped by shepherds in his native Arcadia, god of trading, good
luck and gambling, of divination (he invented sign-systems), of
eloquence, cunning and fraud; and of dream.

Shakespeare's cony-catching rogue (his only lowlife foolish-
wise clown with a Greek name), a reembodiment of this
versatile god, is a wonderful composite of the mercurial and
the picaresque, of failure and recovery. Born under the
appropriate star, "litter'd under Mercury" as he puts it
(IV.iii.25), he is a snapper-up of unconsidered trifles, a singer of
lowlife catches about daffodils and doxies, in which the "red
blood reigns in (reins in? rains in?) the winter's pale" (4); a
titillator of preposterous fancies about usurers' wives brought
to bed of twenty money-bags at once (263). Never at a loss, he
has been ape-bearer, process-server, puppeteer, impersonator,
gambler, whoremaster; he pinches sheets hanging out to dry
(and anything else that comes in handy); he peddles tawdry
trinkets and bawdy broadsheet ballads with such hypnotic
success that all "senses stuck in ears: you might have pinched
a placket, it was senseless; 'twas nothing to geld a codpiece of a
purse" (IV.iv.610–11); and the last we see of him bodes ill for
his latest patron, or victim – his old acquaintance the
shepherd, newly come into a fortune. He, "having flown over
many knavish professions . . . settled only in rogue" (IV.iii.98–
100), but his *coup de théâtre* in *The Winter's Tale* is to con the
clown by enacting the part of his own victim, in order to rob
him of the money for the raisins and currants, prunes,
pear-pies, rice, nutmeg and ginger for the feast.

Trickster, cutpurse, masquerader, shape-changer – what do
we make of this strangely *gratuitous*, outlaw character, so apt
for his part, yet without, it would seem, a part?

We know that he pleases us; that he marks the transition
from winter to spring and from dire consequences for actions
to lucky improvizations and escapes. He provides what is
desired, reputable or disreputable, markets fancies, images,
caters to and exemplifies the instinctual and uninhibited
appetites. What he feels like doing he does, with the cunning of
disguise and dissimulation and a total disregard for regulatory
conscience. So we see in him a pleasure principle, laxity and

relaxation, and welcome his conduct of us from the repressive world of Sicilian punishments to the compensatory wish-fulfillment of Bohemia. Yet he is a thief. What is a thief doing in Shangri-La? Possibly he is there for the same reason as is Polixenes' rage. In the dream they are harmless and judgment is suspended, but their presence reminds us that harmless surfaces conceal explosive depths.

Critics, reading the play and read by it, have recorded contradictory responses in interesting ways. He is a harbinger of spring, says Northrop Frye, "imaginary cuckoo where Leontes is imaginary cuckold" ((1963) 1971, 333). Traversi, more sentimental, finds in him an "affirmation of the warm, living 'blood' of youth against the jealousy and care-laden envy of age"; his song represents the "tender, reborn heart of the year"; his vitality saves the play from abstraction (1965, 136–7). For Tillyard, on the other hand, he is delinquent but "prophylactic," "his delinquencies keep the earthly paradise sufficiently earthly" ((1938) in Kermode, 1938, 84). For Lawlor too, he "offsets any unrealities of pastoral" ((1962) in Palmer, 1971, 300). One might add that the ballads he purveys to the village girls are not without a certain polyphonic relation to the fancies Leontes has entertained. One tells of a monstrous birth, how "a usurer's wife was brought to bed of twenty money-bags at a burden"; another of a fish-woman "turned into a cold fish for she would not exchange flesh with one that loved her" (IV.iv.263, 279). Most comprehensive perhaps is Joan Hartwig's formulation: "Autolycus absorbs some of the disordering aspects of Leontes' disturbed imagination. . . . contain[s] disorder through comic inconsequence" (1978, 101). In sum: Autolycus is a figure of libido, unruly, lawless and volatile, uninhibited, cunning, subversive. Harmless, even benign sometimes, however reluctantly, he offers a semilegiti-mized illicit enjoyment; but there is a self, and a wolf also, in his name.

He is a pervasive presence in the wishful Bohemian scenes, but he is demoted in Sicily, where he must seek preferment under the patronage of the new "true gentlemen" clowns (V.ii.162). Act V deserts the pastoral fantasy to return to the world. There Leontes' restoration is figured, not by dream, but by the art of drama.

The statue scene is the culminating moment of the play. It is carefully prepared for by a cumulative series of encounters, all but the first reported, in order, I suggest, not to detract from the climax, but also to establish the latter's peculiar difference.

A mode of transference takes place in these encounters. The old traumas are reactivated, lived through again, the old wrongs done "stir afresh" within Leontes (V.i.148–9): the death of Hermione: "She I kill'd? I did so; but thou strik'st me/Sorely, to say I did. It is as bitter/Upon thy tongue as in my thought" (16–9); the childhood twinship:

Were I but twenty-one,
Your father's image is so hit in you,
(His very air) that I should call you brother,
As I did him, and speak of something wildly
By us performed before   (126–30)

the loss of his children: "O! alas/I lost a couple that 'twixt heaven and earth/Might thus have stood, begetting wonder" (131–3); the threat to a "gracious couple" through betrayal.

The old desires too. Leontes' instant attraction to Perdita (in the source story resulting in actual incest), which requires Paulina's stern monitoring to deflect, is touching because of the daughter's resemblance to her mother, but it is again threatening. If then Leontes desired a lost mother, and now desires, though unknowingly, his daughter, he is not yet out of the wood. Yet, remembering Autolycus, are we not to see that this piecing together of a dismembered whole – a family, a mind – depends upon the resurgence of desire which is itself beneficent. The reunions are not merely a return of the oppressive past, a nostalgia. The children are as "welcome hither, as is the spring to th'earth" (151–2):

What might I have been,
Might I a son and daughter now have look'd on,
Such goodly things as you!   (176–8)

These recognition scenes are as yet partial. Leontes first

recognizes Polixenes' son in the encounter with the young lovers; then Perdita's identity is discovered in the meeting between all three and Polixenes. This second scene *narrates* the finding of the King's daughter with all the oratorical art the third gentleman can muster:

> Sorrow wept to take leave of them, for their joy waded in tears. . . . Our king, being ready to leap out of himself for joy of his found daughter, as if that joy were now become a loss, cries, 'O, thy mother, thy mother!'; then asks Bohemia forgiveness, then embraces his son-in-law; then again worries he his daughter with clipping her. Now he thanks the old shepherd . . . . I never heard of such another encounter, which lames report to follow it, and undoes description to do it (V.ii.45–62, passim)

and the whole series is parodied by the counterpoint drollery of the clown's version of these wondrously moving events:

> For the King's son took me by the hand and call'd me brother; and then the two kings call'd my father brother; and then the Prince, my brother, and the Princess, my sister, call'd my father father; and so we wept; and there was the first gentlemanlike tears that ever we shed. (140–5)

Only then is the culmination of these reunions brought about in the final scene. Shakespeare's self-reflexive art in the earlier comedies had constantly called attention to itself by means of metadramatic comment and epilogue: we recall Theseus' "The best in this kind are but shadows," and Puck's riposte, "If we shadows have offended." Now we are offered a *tour de force* in the kind, under the sign of Paulina's wildly anachronistic "rare Italian master," and the *trompe-l'oeil* of illusionist art.

Guilio Romano, "who, had he himself eternity and could put breath into his work, would beguile Nature of her custom, so perfectly he is her ape" (92–100) is the creator of Hermione's "statue," the instrument of Paulina's bogus miracle, and, artist as con-man, the *genius loci* of the play's closing phase, as Autolycus was of its wishful dream.

Guilio Romano was a famous mannerist artist of the sixteenth century. In Vasari's *Lives* his Latin epitaph is as follows: "Jupiter saw sculptured and painted statues breathe and earthly buildings made equal to those in heaven by the skill of Giulio Romano" (see Schanzer, 1969, 230). There are good reasons, therefore, for Paulina's (or Shakespeare's) choice, though the entire reference to Romano, has been found pointless. "We do not need his kind of art," says Northrop Frye, "when we have the real Hermione . . . neither he nor the kind of realism he represents seems to be very central to the play itself" (1963, 113). But, I submit, it is central. Because the bogus miracle is a mask for the remedial therapy of Paulina.

The magical effect is made possible by the concealment from the audience of the fact that Hermione is alive. Such concealment is rare in Shakespeare, and its effect is to pull the audience perforce into the experience, making it "real" in a distinctive way: we really see what Leontes sees. The point I am making is that it is a mirror-image of Romano's illusionist skill. Romano's craft made statues so real-seeming that they seemed real persons. Paulina has made a real person so statuesque as to seem a statue. There is of course, no miracle at all. Hermione, never dead, is not resurrected, but what we are shown – Leontes' transport of mingled anguish and joy at its lifelikeness, and then its descent from the pedestal – feels as miraculous, and mysterious, as a return from death or as a birth. We are truly deluded, momentarily, with Leontes. Leontes anticipated a frozen image from the past – "not so much wrinkled, nothing/So aged as this seems" (V.iii.28–9) – with which, perhaps, to prolong and memorialize his stony remorse, to perpetuate nostalgia. This moment creates an illusion of resurrection for Hermione, for Leontes, which is a true *coup de théâtre*, a triumph of the illusionist's art. But the fictive resurrection of Hermione effects a real resurrection in Leontes. Fantasy is transformed into reality as the lost is found. The enchanting moment carries us beyond illusion or deception. It is an embodiment of return – the always unimaginable, the always imagined desire.

When Hermione steps down from the pedestal she is not

only a wifely, but a maternal presence. Though she embraces him first, her first words are for her daughter. She is the agent of his rebirth, of his enfranchisement from the sprites and goblins that haunted him when he was death-possessed, seeing only the skull beneath the skin. It is surely not fortuitous, but a wheel come full circle, when Leontes remembers her "as tender/As infancy" (26–7) and has recourse to an image of primal need, of primal containment and content to express the fullness of his joy "If this be magic, let it be an art/Lawful as eating" (110–1). It is an odd simile, taken at face value. Yet how powerfully resonant it becomes when it can be seen in the chain of signifiers which allow us to reconstruct the untold story of *The Winter's Tale*. Consider the primal oral fantasies which erupted in the tragic phase of the play: the spider-poisoned cup which made Leontes "crack his gorge . . . with violent hefts" (II.i.44–5); the "bespiced" cup which will give his enemy "a lasting wink" (I.ii.316–17); Hermione's provocative "cram's with praise, and make's/As fat as tame things" (I.ii.91–2). Voracious bears and devouring seas accompany the catastrophe. In Bohemia Perdita is "queen of curds and cream" (IV.iv.160), Autolycus steals the money for the festive delicacies which the clown evocatively enumerates, and in his grotesque ballad the usurer's wife "longs to eat adders' heads and toads carbonadoed" (264). Now at last, in Leontes' "lawful as eating," is hunger legitimized, and, no longer signifying a fantasy of incorporation, but a real communion, stilled; family likeness can speak of regeneration, not usurpation, and the existence of others, separate from the shadow play of one's own mind, be acknowledged.

The sprites and goblins are dispersed, but they haunt still, as does, surely, the ghost of Mamillius. The image of gap (Old Norse yawn; a hole or opening made by breaking or parting; a breach) with which *The Winter's Tale* would end the text of its temporal narrative evades closure, evoking not only the fierce disruptions we have witnessed, but beyond these the painful trauma of birth itself, with its continuing, ineluctable, besetting anxieties:[11]

                    Good Paulina,
Lead us from hence, where we may leisurely
Each one demand and answer to his part
Performed in this wide gap of time since first
We were dissevered.   (V.iii.151)

5

Subtleties of the isle: *The Tempest*

Out of the isle, but not of any isle.
Close to the senses there lies another isle
And there the senses give and nothing take,

The opposite of Cythere, an isolation
At the centre . . .

(Wallace Stevens,
"An Ordinary Evening in New Haven," XXI)

The Tempest begins with a shipwreck and ends with an enigma. Neither are what they seem and both are "outside" the dramatic events exhibited during the play, upon the enchanted island. What is "outside," and what is "inside," is indeed one of the matters which is put into question in *The Tempest*, as is the matter of genre itself, and of "play" itself. Unlike its companion romances, which reveal while conceal-ing unconscious shaping fantasies, *The Tempest*, with its magician protagonist, is overtly, manifestly fantastic. It is not the unconscious of the text that the text solicits us to understand, but the consciousness of its wizard stage manager, who gives us advance notice of the nature of the wish fulfillment fantasy he engineers into existence before our eyes.

The fourth and last of the romances brings Shakespearean

tragicomedy to its meridian. It is useful to remember that the German word for comedy is *Lustspiel*, or pleasure play, as Freud pointed out in *Creative Writers and Daydreaming*; for tragedy, *Trauerspiel*, or mourning play. Comedy, exorcist in its function, remedial of errors and follies, obeys the pleasure principle in its gratification of wishes for an imagined happiness, at least an amelioration of human bondage. It provides what is lacking – a mate, wisdom, a community; good luck, good humor, good will. Tragedy presses beyond the pleasure principle to encounter, even to embrace death, yet also to affirm the value of an individual consciousness, dying in its own way. *The Tempest* is a pleasure play, surely? Yet its undercurrent is deeply melancholy, its ending elegiac – "despair," for Prospero, the epilogue says, "Unless [he] be reliev'd by prayer." What is the nature of this momentum in the play towards death – "Every third thought . . . my grave" (V.i.311) synchronic with its movement towards, and fulfillment of, a rejoicing "Beyond a common joy" (207)?

The Tempest invites reflection upon the relation between Freud and Shakespeare at a number of points of convergence. It is possible to construct a kind of intertextual dialogue between these two observers of the human scene. The dialogue I have in mind is not, however, with Freud the exegetical detective, diagnostician and therapist, but rather with Freud the meta-psychologist, the anthropologist and philosopher of civilization and its discontents. *The Tempest* is corrective of the negative thrust of *Creative Writers and Daydreaming*, containing what the latter lacks in its failure to credit the artist's creation with more than the provision of diversionary pleasure to distract the secondary, reality-testing processes of the mind, while the primary processes of autistic fantasy can be safely released, and dispelled. *The Tempest* exhibits fantasy neither as merely libidinous nor as defensive, but as heuristic; and it is never deluded. *The Tempest* imagines a process of maturation, of sublimation, of renunciation; the relinquishing of needs, passions, bonds, possessivenesses which are regressive and enslaving, for the attaining of eudaemonic ends; but it also imagines the struggle of their attaining, and its limits.

What does this pleasure play tell us of pleasure, of power, safety, liberty, the quest of all its dramatis personae? Prospero found these in a cell in Milan, where his library was "dukedom large enough" (I.ii.110) until his deputy brother usurped his place and cast him out to sea; Alonso found them in regal power, until the loss of his son. Antonio, who would "have no screen between this part he play'd/And him he play'd it for" and must be therefore "Absolute Milan" (107-9), in narcissistic aggrandizement; Gonzalo, provider of food, fresh water, garments, beloved books to the castaways, found them in charity; Miranda and Ferdinand in love; Stephano and Trinculo in the oblivion and the intoxication of the bottle; Caliban in creature comforts, the immediate gratification of the primal instinctual cravings; and Ariel in a cowslip. The animating fantasy of *The Tempest* is itself embedded in Prospero's name: it is a grand design for happiness snatched out of disaster, not least the disaster of being born human. The shipwreck figures disaster, but Prospero's conjuring trick shipwreck constitutes a rebirth for the survivors, who believe themselves rescued. "Not so much perdition as a hair" (30) is suffered by any of the voyagers, not so much as a blemish is to be seen upon their sustaining garments when they find themselves alive and ashore. Dazed, amazed, bewitched by strange sounds and sweet airs, by apparitions and hallucinations, they pursue, like banished Kent, their old courses in a country new, but this time under a monitoring eye, and wand.

This – Prospero's magicianship – is the secondary organizing fantasy of *The Tempest*, a fantasy of omnipotence, whereby the crooked shall be made straight and all manner of things be well. Isaiah's redemptive latter-day fantasy (and Noah's, another survivor) hovers over the language of *The Tempest* in many places even if Ariel's name did not come from chapter 29. Charles K. Hofling (1974) makes the interesting point that the King James Bible was completed in 1611, and that in addition to the name Ariel, nine thematically relevant phrases, images and ideas that occur in Isaiah 29, such as vengeance, a familiar spirit, storm and tempest, a flame of devouring fire, dream, drunkenness and deep sleep recur in *The Tempest*. One could add a sealed book of wisdom, and the doing of a marvelous work. If Shakespeare was reading or rereading the Bible, as well as the Bermuda pamphlets, in 1611, and thinking perhaps about Noah, he might well have remembered the story of Noah's daughters, who, for lack of any alternative on the desert island of Ararat, knew their father. Other biblical daughters had occurred to him in the past: Jephtah's, for instance, in *Hamlet*, and Leah, married to Jacob through a bed-trick, it will be recalled, in *The Merchant*.

The beauty of *The Tempest* is that the fantasy is reality-tested within its own confines. Prospero's civilizing enterprise on Sycorax' island is brought face to face with its own discontents, its own mal-contents.

Let us examine Prospero's grand design.

Prospero, we are informed, was never a man ambitious for worldly power. Already in Milan he had neglected "worldly ends" for the "secret studies" which would further "the bettering of [his] mind" (I.ii.89–90) while Antonio was given the office of his deputy. Insulated – enisled – in the quest for the mind's power "to liberate the soul from the passions,"[1] Prospero believes that his own defection from ducal responsibility awoke the "evil nature" in his ambitious brother, whose native malice and arrogance, however, we have already glimpsed in the crisis of the storm. The island magnifies and clarifies the attributes of both these manipulative, if dialectically opposed sibling rivals. The island events are their designs for living writ large.

For fifteen years in this island sanctuary Prospero has lived in intimate seclusion with his daughter, a seclusion untroubled and uninterrupted save by the island creature Caliban's attempt upon her. This daughter, whose presence as a babe in the rotten bark saved him from despair, whom he has bred and loved and taught, now presents him with a drastic double bind. She must now herself be saved, (they both must be) from the loveliest of all fantasies. To live thus, father and daughter, alone and together, with no rival to challenge, no rebellion to threaten, no sexual turmoil to overthrow the beatific enjoyment of beauty, of obedience, of affection, of consideration (she really is the perfect daughter!) in loving reciprocity and perfect harmony – what is this but the wishful fantasy of a Lear, who would sing like a bird in a cage in prison with Cordelia, or the fantasy of any parent: a revivified, reintensified primal unity with the child who replaces his or her own lost good parent. It might amuse one to reflect that such would have been, presumably, the wishful fantasy of all the thwarting and defied fathers in the Terentian comedies, had the plots of those plays allowed them to figure in their own right, as it were, rather than simply as an obstacle to the mating of the young.[2] However, as Barber pointed out long ago (1969), where the early comedies are designed to free sexuality from the bonds of family, the romances are engaged in freeing parental love from the threat of sexuality. So even on Prospero's island, particularly on Prospero's civilized island, these revels must come to an end; for Miranda is fifteen, nubile and marriagable, and Prospero's time, under the shadow of the threat, under the shadow of Caliban's constant reminder, is running out. He must find a match for his daughter. He must end what he longs to prolong.

The famous first dialogue between Prospero and Miranda, in which he nags for her attention, neatly provides necessary information but also dramatizes Prospero's sense of urgency, of a moment which is now ripe, and of a hidden import of the nature of which he cannot enlighten his interlocutor.[3] The stars in their courses have brought about a propitious conjunction – his "zenith" (etymologically road, way or path) depends upon a "most auspicious star" (I.ii.181–2). The King of Naples is on his way home from his daughter's marriage. In Prospero's mind a plan has crystallized, a transcendent design for the resolution of all problems, moral and practical. He will marry his daughter to no other than the son of the King of Naples, who, since Antonio's betrayal, is the overlord of Milan. He will thus undo, and outdo, Antonio's treachery: his heirs, not Antonio's, will rule Milan. Gonzalo, rejoicing "beyond a common joy" at the play's conclusion, makes the point: "Was Milan thrust from Milan, that his issue/Should become kings of Naples?" (V.i.205–7) This marriage, then, between Miranda and Ferdinand will be the sweetest and subtlest of all possible matches and revenges, hoisting Antonio with his own petard and yet sanctified by its obviously beneficent purpose. Is it revenge? Or is it revenge so sublimated as to lose the name of revenge? It is no wonder that he is excited, that he relishes every detail of the smooth execution, is delighted with the performance of his "brave spirit" Ariel, is still more delighted when "it works," his plan, and Miranda and Ferdinand are instantly attracted to each other. When he then plays the classic *senex*, staging a tyrannical ferocity, throwing suspicion upon Ferdinand, magically disarming him of his sword, enslaving him to log-chopping, he announces these impositions as tests of Ferdinand's character, "lest too light winning/ Make the prize light" (I.ii.452–3). However, it is not difficult to perceive in these metaphorical castrations the symbolic enactment of what, albeit repressed, will still out: a possessive father's hostility to his usurper rival.

Prospero's progress throughout the play is a Herculean contest with himself, with ambivalence. What he does, with regard to Miranda's betrothal, he would dearly love to undo. What he forgives, with regard to Antonio's usurpation, he would dearly love to avenge. Prospero does not suddenly discover that "the rarer action is/In virtue than in vengeance" (V.i.27–8), for this, as an enlightened prince, he knows from the start. It is a communal, and his own, ideal of conduct. What he has to do is to realize his knowledge in action and feeling, but he is filled with love for his beloved daughter, and he is filled with rage against his perfidious brother. These are imperious passions, as hard to subdue as Caliban is to tame; the primal energies, erotic and vindictive. Simply, massively, to repress them, as a man of strict and icy conscience, would make of Prospero an Angelo, an armour-plated, fragile and unhappy man. Simply to indulge them would reduce the great project of civility to naturalist abandon, and make of him another Antonio.

Prospero, unlike Duke Vincentio, his precursor, has supernatural power at his disposal, and spirits to command. He is entirely in charge. He can stage-manage events, create storms at sea, conjure up visions, manipulate situations and people. His actions, therefore, are his wishes, his wishes his actions; but it doesn't always quite work out according to plan. His captives get a little out of hand at times, putting *him* to the test, and this is the course of the play's dramatic tension: formal artifice – shows, emblems, didactic object lessons are constantly destabilized by unpremeditated contingencies, spontaneity which occurs despite the magical control. Total power is exhibited and defeated at once.

Structurally, *The Tempest* is a play within a play: Prospero's, within Shakespeare's, or, one is sometimes tempted to fancy, Shakespeare's within Prospero's. The embedding of play within play dissolves representational boundaries so that the audience is required to suspend its attention, to negotiate a constant interchange between fictional reality and fictional illusion: Prospero creates happenings by having the volatile and tricksy spirit, Ariel, bewilder, placate or punish his captives with shows, which are illusions. The island's enchantments are Prospero's inventions but they are realities for the play's personae; the beings who inhabit the island are indeterminately human and phantasmagoric, as the absurdities of the comic passages ludicrously underline. *The Tempest*'s mingled yarn dramatizes heuristic fantasy: *The Tempest* is a day-dream in which Prospero, spectator at his own show, remembers and reconstructs, recalls past threats (which then repeat themselves, once in deadly earnest, once in comic parody) and fantasizes (or realizes?) a reordering of his life. Only in the wedding entertainment is the show overtly, and with the knowledge of the play-spectators, a masque, and that, as we shall see, is dissolved, as were masques in real life, into the realities of the final recognition scenes.

In dreams, as we know, opposites obtain. Going is coming, finding is bringing, banishment may represent a deep wish for flight, log-chopping displaces a threat of castration; and opposites are split off internal objects, or imagos. Prospero found Ariel and Caliban on the island which was Sycorax's, but the embedding of narration within narration makes the journey to that fabulous location a journey into a psychic interior[3] and we readily understand them as representing some emotional or mental aspect of Prospero himself. Prospero replaced the witch Sycorax (a reincarnation of Circe, transformer of men into beasts, according to the Arden editor (Kermode, 1962, 26)) – his own malign double. She too, like himself, was banished, with a child, and abandoned upon the island; her black sorcery is the barbarous counterpart to his theurgic magic. Releasing Ariel, "too delicate/To act her earthy and abhorr'd commands" (I.ii.272–3) from imprisonment in a cloven pine, he incarcerates her favored son Caliban and imposes upon him (as later upon Ferdinand) log-bearing slavery. Replacing the bad mother, he is a father to them both, scolding, castigating, punishing, teaching. Prospero turns ferociously upon Ariel when the latter objects to yet another task. "Malignant thing," he scolds, "dull thing" (257, 285), and threatens punishment of exactly the kind meted out by Sycorax: "I will rend an oak/And pen thee in his knotty entrails till/Thou hast howl'd away twelve winters" (294–6). The antithetical symmetries of the symbolic foursome are central to Shakespeare's invention, which, I suggest, performs nothing less than the figuring forth of what we now call the unconscious. These imaginative creations embody desires, memories, impulses not available to cognitive conceptualization, but only to an intuition of primary tensions, primary duality. Through them a path is opened into the infinite regress of repetition compulsion, of amnesia, "the dark backward and abysm of time" (50) as Prospero memorably puts it.[4]

Shakespeare had precursors in the allegorical personification of the psyche: Marlowe's good and evil angels, the whole of Spenser's master work, the medieval allegorists; and he has had successors, in Jung, and in Freud, who have capitalized, each in his own way, upon his insights. However, his own is its unique and inimitable self, and is not collapsible into any other. Let us attempt to elucidate the allegories of Ariel and Caliban.

The temptation to construe Prospero as ego and Ariel and Caliban as superego and id (or anima and animus/animal[5]) replaces the more traditional readings of the kind formulated by Marjorie Garber, namely Prospero as mankind or poet, Ariel imagination, Caliban natural or instinctive man (1974). It has been taken up by several psychoanalytically oriented interpretors,[6] most recently by Meredith Skura. "Freud internalized Shakespeare's dramas," she says. His metapsychological theories resemble Shakespeare's plays "since they anthropomorphize the parts of the mind, as does Shakespeare . . . Ariel and Caliban may be seen as walking portraits of 'the conscious' and the 'unconscious'" (1981, 36–7, passim). There is something troubling about these ascriptions however. It is easy to see the mastering, controlling, adaptational ego-functions in Prospero, and an id-figure in the idle, lustful, piggish, resentful (and enslaved) Caliban, who exhibits what the Renaissance would have regarded as a natural profanity needing constantly to be tamed and restrained in the degree that it cannot be enlightened,[7] but superego demands, strictures, moral imperatives seem to belong more to Prospero than to the pliant and metamorphic, playful and freedom-loving Ariel. The attempt to cut Shakespeare's cloth precisely according to Freudian specification meets with too many obstacles in the dramatization of *The Tempest* to be anything but procrustean. Shakespeare's "other scene" was not Freud's. Freud's discoveries can rediscover for us much that is embodied in Shakespeare's; but Shakespeare's, in their turn, can amplify Freud's.

Prospero's fantasy of omnipotence, his dialogue with Miranda suggests, included the desire to be an onlie begetter, prolific and nourishing. Antonio "new created/The creatures that were mine" (I.ii.81–2) he says resentfully; Antonio became an ivy which "sucked my verdure out" (87). Such grandiose omnipotence, psychoanalytical theory tells us, is a defense against its obverse, the infantile terror of total dependency, therefore it requires the fantasied destruction of maternal power. Miranda, it will be recalled, sees no mother figure in the dim past of her memory, only vague women attendants; later she says that she remembers "no woman's face" save her own in her mirror (III.i.49–51). There is, indeed, a notable absence, or repression, of mothers in *The Tempest*. "The mother aspect of woman is under a peculiar tabu," says Abenheimer (Faber, 1970, 515) who sees both Miranda and Ariel as fantasized beneficent surrogate feminine presences. But this absence of mothers would be true of the middle comedies too, with their resourceful and adventurous heroines. In *The Tempest* there is a mother – the witch-mother Sycorax – "with age and envy/. . . grown into a hoop" (I.ii.257–8), a female claw, an evil female dominance which is annihilated, since she dies before the opening of the play. Is Sycorax then a derivative of infantile fantasy, a bad mother upon whom the helpless rage and terror of separation is projected? In this connection we note the imagery of the oceanic, pervasive in *The Tempest*, especially in the echoing, haunting compounds – sea-sorrow, sea-storm, sea-swallowed, sea-change – which are peculiar to this play, and, though subdued to an undertone by comparison with *Pericles* – for Prospero is endowed with a power over storms at sea rather than a Gower to narrate his proneness to fall a victim to them – the swallowing and belching sea is, from the first graphic scene of the wreck, a constant verbal evocation. It is possible to read in *The Tempest* polyphonic variations upon the theme of a lifetime's contest with the oceanic.

But to return from the ego of Prospero to his pair of servitors: if we try to map the Freudian metapsychology upon the Shakespearean, we can see that the latter extends the range of meanings implicit in the former as generally received. Ariel, rather than being a superego (with the connotations, not only of "ego-ideal" but of a censorious, critical and punitive function), or "the conscious" (for what is then left to ego?), represents, I suggest, the urge towards sublimation, and Caliban the drift towards regression – a Shakespearean Eros and Thanatos respectively – and it is the struggle between these two cardinal impulses that structures the progress of the play, and can mediate our understanding of it, especially of the angers of Prospero, which have proved a stumbling block to interpreters.

His vituperation of Ariel – "Malignant thing . . . dull thing" (I.ii.257, 285) occurs after the capturing of the ship's party has been splendidly accomplished with "not a hair perish'd"; the next step in Prospero's project is, significantly, the leading of Ferdinand to Miranda, crux of the renunciation that he must effectuate. If Ariel fails him now his entire project crumbles. The moment Ariel has capitulated and flown off to become the water-nymph whose invisible beguilements will bring Ferdinand from the sea-shore where he sits mourning his father's loss, we are introduced to Caliban, the "poisonous slave got by the devil himself" (319), "hagseed," "freckled whelp," "filth," "earth," once the recipient of Prospero's affection, and guide to the island's fertile bounty, now object of his unmitigated hatred and contempt. The wonderfully imagined pair, linked and opposed, loved and hated, recalcitrant and obedient, mirror Prospero's complex ambivalence: he both wills to annul or to transcend the natural craving for destructive revenge, to transform and so in some way to preserve the naturally exclusive attachment to Miranda, and is tempted to yield to that which is to be transformed and transcended.

Both Prospero's creatures are marvelously imagined: Ariel, spirit of transformation, invisible to the audience except in his various transformations, sublimated agent of Prospero's grand scheme of sublimations, and regressive Caliban, stubbornly a presence precivilized, uninhibited, abhorred and feared, hence object of Prospero's own sadistic rage. Ariel, all air and fire – elements of sublimation in alchemy – Prospero's "Delicate Ariel" (I.ii.442), his "bird" (IV.i.184), is etherealized, spiritualized, hermaphrodite; Caliban, earth and fen-water, half brute half demon, is grossly, aggressively male, but rendered impotent under Prospero's domination. Sexuality is strictly under guard on Prospero's island, as he warns Ferdinand, repeatedly. It was precisely Caliban's attempt to rape Miranda, it will be recalled, which lost him Prospero's original affection and earned instead the cramps and aches and pinches and blisters with which he is tormented, by, among other means, creatures appropriately spiky and snaky ("hedgehogs which/Lie tumbling in my barefoot way, and mount/Their pricks at my footfall . . . adders, who with cloven tongues/Do hiss me into madness" (II.ii.10–14)).

Norman Holland ((1964) 1970, 522ff.) has picked out the imagery suggestive of infantile libido in his analysis of Trinculo's discovery of the "deboshed fish" Caliban in the monster shape on the shore: "Yond same black cloud, yond huge one, looks like a foul bumbard that would shed his liquor" (II.ii.20–2) parodies in advance, he says, Caliban's dream of a sensorily soporific, pleasure-providing environment: "Be not afeard," Caliban says to Stephano, his fellow conspirator made nervous by Ariel's audible invisibility:

> the isle is full of noises,
> Sounds, and sweet airs, that give delight and hurt not.
> Sometimes a thousand twangling instruments
> Will hum about mine ears; and sometimes voices,
> That if I then had wak'd after long sleep,
> Will make me sleep again, and then in dreaming,
> The clouds methought would open, and show riches
> Ready to drop upon me, that when I wak'd
> I cried to dream again.   (III.ii.135–43)

This fantasy is surely derivative – a palimpsest of a child between sleep and waking with his thumb in his mouth. Trinculo crawls under the shape's fishy-smelling gaberdine, only to be discovered by Stephano as a fourlegged monster with two mouths, one before and one behind, into both of which he happily pours his bottle of "riches" (II.ii.88–93). "In effect," says Holland, "shortly before Caliban tells his new-found masters his recurring dream, they have recited and acted out for him a 'black,' 'foul,' smelly, and backward – in short, anal – version of that dream" (526). The drunken butler and his jester colleague (themselves childish) uncover, from an alienated adult but comically good-tempered point of view, the primordial infant in the primitive savage with the voracious name.

Upon Prospero Caliban hurls malignant curses which are reciprocated with punitive vindictiveness, for they are engaged in mortal combat, these two, as a man with his most inward and intimate threat. It is the threat of a return of the repressed, of the *bête noir*, the thing of darkness which accounts for Prospero's rage at the height of the festivities when he recalls

the "foul conspiracy/Of the beast Caliban and his confeder-
ates" (IV.i.139–40), an episode which has seemed superfluous
and unaccountable to many commentators. It is a far cry from
innocent orality or anality, even from less innocent greed and
lust to the raw uninhibited pursuit of murder and rape,
however disabused of actual menace these may be; but the
latter are what he has to contend with as he walks away "to
still [his] beating mind" (163). It "beats in his mind." The
phrase recurs like a pulse.

If Caliban is imagined as infantile, shape-changing Ariel,
affectionate, docile, playful, volatile, is childlike, representing
a wishful fantasy rooted in the same primal soil. Ariel's "sweet
airs" allay the fury and the passion of Ferdinand, "weeping
again the King [his] father's wrack" (I.ii.391, 393–4). "Come
unto these yellow sands" invites its dancers to curtsy, kiss, and
"foot it featly" while the "wild waves" are calmed, the sun
shines, the protective watch-dog barks and the barnyard cock
crows (375–87). If this is an invitation to the dance, proleptic of
Ferdinand's fortunes on the island, it is also a nursery rhyme.
Ariel's final song, in Act V, scene i, as he anticipates his
freedom, is a kind of lullaby in its evocation of ease and safety,
its transformation of womb or breast into a cowslip's bell, its
intimacy, the delicate eroticism of its miniscule cowslips and
blossoms, and its friendly creatures:

> Where the bee sucks, there suck I,
> In a cowslip's bell I lie;
> There I couch when owls do cry.
> On the bat's back I do fly
> After summer merrily.
> Merrily, merrily shall I live now,
> Under the blossom that hangs on the bough.   (88–94)

"Full fathom five," the most haunting of these lyrics of
recreation, transforms death itself, refashions mortal remains,
watches the never-surfeited sea metamorphose skeletons into
coral and eyeballs into pearls, forbids mourning:

> Full fadom five thy father lies,

Of his bones are coral made:
Those are pearls that were his eyes:
  Nothing of him that doth fade,
But doth suffer a sea-change
Into something rich and strange.
Sea-nymphs hourly ring his knell.   (I.ii.397–403)

These pearls and corals – transitional objects which defend against grief, loss, dissolution – are apotropaic. They preserve and immortalize, by the transformations of a mythic natural alchemy. Themselves the work of the sea's living organisms, they are a trope, says Marjorie Garber, "for the activity of artistic creation" (1974, 141). It has been my argument that that trope is itself a trope, in *The Tempest*, for the activity of psychic reformation. It is upon himself that Prospero works his wizardry, and it is the vicissitudes of the creative imagination that Ariel and Caliban illuminate.

Anne Barton claims that *The Tempest* "is an extraordinarily secretive work of art . . . deliberately enigmatic . . . [seeming] to hide as much as it reveals" and depending to a "surprising" extent upon "the suppressed and the unspoken," upon fragmentary and disjointed glimpses of "a vitally important past" that the dramatist "did not choose to elucidate . . . . It provokes imaginative activity on the part of its audience or readers. . . . demand[s] interpretation and expansion" (1980, 12–26, passim). To the extent that these observations apply to all great works of literature they apply to *The Tempest*, but the inner dimension of *The Tempest* is actually less veiled or occulted than in the other romances because we are privy to the protagonist's will and intentions from the outset, at least from scene ii. Other plays provide screens for fantasies which reveal themselves in devious ways. Here Prospero announces his wishful intention from the start, which, since it depends upon his possession of magic powers is necessarily already in the realm of fantasy. The apparitions, mysteries, "strangenesses" are experienced as such by the manipulated dramatis personae, not the audience, who are, with Prospero, in the know.

Nevertheless we have still to read, to spell out, Prospero's fantasy as the play's dynamic articulates it.

We can understand Antonio as a figure out of a fifteen-year-old past who reappears and is reencountered, in a reenactment of his original malfeasance; but we can also understand him as Prospero's *alter ego*. Like other sibling rivals in Shakespeare, including Alonso and Sebastian in this very play, they are split, antithetical, decomposed parts of a psychic whole. Both sought power, one by grasping, one by withdrawing. Both would be "absolute Milan" (I.ii.109), but one renounces, or sublimates, one ruthlessly fulfills the passions and appetites of the mind. Antonio's "sleepy language" to Sebastian (II.i.211) parallels Prospero's enchantments in that both are machiavellian and manipulative, both seek the end of contemplative magic, namely, to cause changes in consciousness by the exercise of will; but Prospero is good, and Antonio is evil – in psychological terms, one represents the compensatory, reparative urge, the other the envious and destructive. There are few villains in Shakespeare more heartlessly, chillingly cynical than Antonio and Sebastian. If the exhibition of Antonio's villainy is a test for Prospero, audiences are certainly enabled to sympathize. What auditor has not wished something very unpleasant, and quite unsublimated, to happen to the jeering pair?

The five scenes of Acts II and III divide symmetrically between the court party sophisticates and the fools, with the scene between the lovers, watched by Prospero, forming the apex of a triangle: court-party, fools, lovers, fools, court-party. The courtiers appear in Act II, structurally the phase which articulates the terms of the drama's psychomachia. They anchor the contest between the better and the worse human possibilities in the concrete actualities of political behavior, just as Gonzalo's Montaignean Golden-Age dream of effortless natural bounty, security, untroubled and perpetual plenitude translates Caliban's dream, and Ariel's, into terms of property and polity. Gonzalo is mercilessly mocked by the cynics, but the conspiracy of Antonio and Sebastian is itself mocked by Stephano's parody of a plot, as is their intoxication by the foolish glee of the inebriated and self-enslaved Caliban.

Shakespeare's employment here of fool parody is a return to his high mastery of the mode in the mature comedies: the fools' doings ridicule the aspirations of the middle characters, while enhancing those of the higher – in this case morally rather than socially higher – protagonists.[8] Stephano floating ashore on his wine-butt is a survivor of the tempest, like Noah-Prospero, and a colonizer-king (to Caliban), which mocks the would-be usurpers. The villains have their banquet – another dream of satiety – ludicrously snatched from them at the play's reversal. Note, however, the modulation of register that follows:

> You fools! I and my fellows
> Are ministers of Fate . . .
>   your swords . . . may as well
> Wound the loud winds, or with bemock't-at stabs
> Kill the still-closing waters, as diminish
> One dowle that's in my plume.   (III.iii.60–5)

The fierce female bird-monster's denunciation of the "three men of sin" (53) precipitates, at least in Alonso, a gnawing remorse which exacerbates his grief for his son till he can only desire to end his own life, "mudded" – no sea-change here – in the ooze where his son is bedded.

Whether sinister, or comic, or solemn, the alternations of Acts II and III, and the central scene of the lovers' vows are a sustained dramatic meditation upon the themes of subservience and mastery, guilt and liberation, the better and the worse of the human possibilities. Three times in these scenes is a coupling watched. The tipsy Stephano, who later takes the mooncalf under his fatherly wing, observes the extremely strange coupling of two mouths and four legs in the composite "monster" under the gaberdine (II.ii.89). The villainous brothers watch the sleeping pair of vulnerable older figures, Alonso and Gonzalo, related anagrammatically as they are related by guilt and goodness respectively, and plan their speedy demise (II.i.198–296); and Prospero watches the love-exchange between Miranda and Ferdinand, the crown of his scheme, with a complex ambivalence. "Poor worm, thou art infected" (III.i.31) he says, but also, "Fair encounter/Of two most rare affections! Heavens rain grace/On that which breed between 'em!" (74–6). There is a wry self-awareness in the balance-sheet of his summing up:

> So glad of this as they I cannot be,
> Who are surpris'd [withal] but my rejoicing
> At nothing can be more.   (92–4)

By Act IV Prospero's design and the foiling of the villains is all but completed. It remains to "bestow upon the eyes of [the] young couple/Some vanity of [his] art" (IV.i.40–1), before the discovery of the truth which will bring about the recuperation of the repentant sinners, and the conclusion of his project. Re-creation, renunciation, recognition, regeneration, and then return. Prospero's morality play is faultlessly conceived and worked out; his self-congratulation surely justified; but the play is not finished, and it is not a play. Prospero, as has been noted, is himself tested by the drama he has imagined.

In a sense the whole of *The Tempest*, the enchanted island itself, represents a version of the pastoral restorative "other place" of liberating fantasy in which Shakespearean comedy is rooted. The remedial fantasy comes to a culmination in the fourth act nuptial masque with its imagery of natural abundance, rural labor and well-being – Prospero works hard at his project of guiding, checking, ordering and re-forming:

> Ceres, most bounteous lady, thy rich leas
> Of wheat, rye, barley, fetches, oats, and pease;
> Thy turfy mountains, where live nibbling sheep,
> And flat meads thatch'd with stover, them to keep;
> Thy banks with pioned and twilled brims,
> Which spungy April at thy hest betrims,
> To make cold nymphs chaste crowns   (IV.i.60–6)

This is a nourishing and nourished land, fertile in contrast to its "sea-marge, sterile and rocky-hard" (69). True, the nymphs are cold, and the bachelors "lass-lorn" (68), but this could be seen as a temporary and necessary stage in the life-history of the young. The question which has been found most troublesome is Prospero's sudden vexation during the betrothal masque in Act IV, which is signalled by "strange, hollow and confused noise" and the vanishing into thin air of the masquers. Miranda has never seen him so "touch'd with anger, so distemper'd" (145). He calls off the "revels" and retires to his cell to "still [his] beating mind" (163). What beats in Prospero's mind?

Let us first consider the masque itself, which he has composed and which therefore will speak his meaning. The three deities are carefully chosen for the nuptial that Prospero has conceived and brought about: Juno, goddess of the rain-bestowing sky, Ceres of the receiving earth, and Iris, the rainbow messenger who joins above and below with promise of a postdiluvian regeneration, a return of the natural cycle of seedtime and harvest. But what of the goddess of Love, whose absence is queried by Ceres herself?

This is after all a wedding ceremony, Venus should surely have a part to play, but Venus and Cupid, who "thought to have done/Some wanton charm" upon the bridal couple, are not among the sponsors of this masque. "Mars's hot minion" was seen safely "cutting the clouds towards Paphos" with her "waspish-headed son" who "has broke his arrows,/Swears he will shoot no more, but play with sparrows/And be a boy right out" (93–101, passim). Chaste fertility was a Renaissance commonplace, premarital sex firmly out of bounds. There is nothing here that is in the least unconventional. Yet the interdict on Venus, and the refusal to contemplate an adult Cupid is emphatic. A fertility ritual which bans sex is odd, and therefore expressive, we may infer, of Prospero's need to ward off sexuality even in the celebration of his daughter's marriage, or particularly in the celebration of his daughter's marriage. "So rare a wond'red father and a wise/Makes this place Paradise" (123–4) says Ferdinand, picking up his father-in-law's own theme of another Genesis. Prospero taught Caliban, it will be recalled, "how/To name the bigger light, and how the less,/That burn by day and night" (I.ii.334–6); Prospero, survivor and maker of floods, entertains the fantasy of a second creation, a new-made world which will be without libido, or will have mastered its force. But the mature and benign fantasy gives way at a moment of crisis to the persecutory anxiety of an earlier desperation.

The masque is disrupted. It breaks off, its spell broken, just at the moment of the dance of the river Naiads with the Reapers. Reapers gather in the harvest, but they are tearers and renders, actually and etymologically, and immemorial signifiers of death. Prospero remembers Caliban, who would have violated his daughter and would do so again if his conspiracy succeeds. And Prospero experiences an upsurge of almost uncontrollable rage.

Prospero's perturbation reveals the core of his emotional problem, as a reading of the symbolic sequence can make clear. The "sunburn'd sicklemen," with their intimations of mortality, and of castration (the scythe of Father Time, Panovsky reminds us, was originally Saturn's castrating sickle before Kronos/Saturn and Chronos/Time were conflated),[9] precipitate the recall of "a born devil, on whose nature/Nurture can never stick" (IV.i.188–9). How can we read this but as a stubborn return of the repressed, of the utterly tabooed, of his own unacknowledged desire, together with the terror that accompanies it and is then unleashed in rage upon Caliban? Caliban is the rock upon which the fantasy of omnipotence and the fantasy of sublimation both founder. The dispiriting fact that Prospero now faces, at this culminating moment, is that he is not, after all, master in his own house. He glimpses beyond the three daughters of Eros, Iris, Juno and Ceres, the three faces of Thanatos: lust and rage and death, that no fantasy can abolish, no mastery control.

He recaptures the self-possession of a host: "You do look, my son, in a mov'd sort,/As if you were dismay'd: be cheerful, sir" (IV.i.146–7); but the whole of the famous speech that ends the revels is a struggle for composure:

> Our revels now are ended. These our actors
> (As I foretold you) were all spirits, and
> Are melted into air, into thin air,
> And like the baseless fabric of this vision,
> The cloud-capp'd tow'rs, the gorgeous palaces,

The solemn temples, the great globe itself,
Yea, all which it inherit, shall dissolve,
And like this insubstantial pageant faded
Leave not a rack behind. We are such stuff
As dreams are made on; and our little life
Is rounded with a sleep. Sir, I am vex'd;
Bear with my weakness, my old brain is troubled.
Be not disturb'd with my infirmity.
If you be pleas'd, retire into my cell,
And there repose. A turn or two I'll walk
To still my beating mind.   (148–63)

It needs no more than an actor's gesture to make the apparently superfluous repetition: "the baseless fabric of this vision," "this insubstantial pageant," refer disjunctively to world and to theater and then to deny the difference. The speech collapses the levels of representation with which *The Tempest* has juggled: the globe that is the world, the Globe that was the theater, fantasy, reality, dream, all are one, a little life islanded in an ocean of nonexistence. "It seems strange," says Northrop Frye, "that a melancholy elegy on the dissolving of all things in time should be the emotional crux of the play" (1959, 10). But is it so strange? The lament for the passing of time is so poignant that it obscures the radical narcissism of which it is the expression. The world disappears with the observing eye only if the I is everything. "They told me I was every thing," said Lear (IV.vi.104), whose very accents can be heard in the last lines of the speech. The speech is as poignant as it is because it captures the primary narcissism of Everyman, with whom and for whom the world begins and ends; the primary yearning, always destined to defeat, for total possession of the beloved other who is also and at once oneself.

Ariel can dowse the would-be conspirators in pools of horse-piss, bedazzle them (the civilized ones, at least) with trumpery, and hound them from the stage, but he (or his master) cannot transform the Caliban in himself:

A devil, a born devil, on whose nature
Nurture can never stick; on whom my pains,

Humanely taken, all, all lost, quite lost;
And as with age his body uglier grows,
So his mind cankers.   (IV.i.188–92)

The lament opens upon an abyss of dismay. It is his own old age, as much as Caliban's, that is envisaged. So he punishes Caliban and company, sadistically, not only with goblin pinches, but with aches and pains from within an aging body:

Go, charge my goblins that they grind their joints
With dry convulsions, shorten up their sinews
With aged cramps, and more pinch-spotted make them
Than pard or cat o'mountain.   (258–61)

In terms of tragic structure this is Prospero's moment of despair, the surrender of his will to make sublimation prevail; but in the recognition scenes of Act V Ariel again comes into his own, when Prospero's captives, entirely in his power, are saved and forgiven.

Then Prospero solemnly dismisses his puppet-elves, buries his staff, drowns his book. He renounces his fantasy of omnipotent domination of nature and men, sets Ariel, "his diligence," his "chick" free. Why? Has he no more need of a sublimating discipline? Of Art? Is happiness so firmly secured as to need no further maintaining? Or is it because Caliban is an ineluctable fact of life, Ariel an evanescent grace? We are not, certainly, asked to believe in a transformation of Antonio, a pat repentance. He is obstinately, or grimly, silent. It is also to be noticed that he (together with Sebastian) is now within Prospero's (natural) power, a permanent hostage to good behavior. "Were I so minded," Prospero addresses his "brace of lords," "I here could pluck his Highness' frown upon you/And justify you traitors. At this time/I will tell no tales" (V.i.126–9). Nor are we required to share Miranda's admiration of "the goodly creatures" of her "brave new world" (V.i.182–3). Prospero, would-be maker of a brave new world, speaks with a total absence of illusion when he says, dryly, "Tis new to thee" (184). Is then the final note of *The Tempest* tragic rather than comic? Have the innumerable commentators who have found

The Tempest the acme of serenity been, perhaps wishfully, deluded?

Yet Prospero has triumphed. Who can deny it? Prospero's fantasy, his Eros design for human amelioration, for human regeneration has achieved its end. He wished to be set free – from his island, from obsessive memories, hatreds, from the past, from the problem of a loved young daughter cut off from human society. All these ends are magnificently accomplished. Yet when he returns to Milan his every third thought will be the grave. He is stirred, unhappy, in a way that suggests that the beating in his mind is unassuaged; and at the end, in the famous epilogue, which unmasks the fictional protagonist to reveal the professional actor pleading for the plaudits of an actual audience and which recognizes the play's make-believe, its consolatory fantasy, by drawing attention to it, he pleads, as if all is to be done again, to be set free. Why, and from what "bands" does he now long to be released?

Prospero, with a great effort of renunciation, has created the conditions for happiness on his island but he cannot, as cynical Sebastian knows "carry this island home in his pocket, and give it his son for an apple" (II.i.91–2). Prospero knows what the cynics know, and more. He knows that his triumph is a triumph because, and in so far as the perennial force of the instinctual – of what he has overcome – is recognized. "This thing of darkness I acknowledge mine" (V.i.275) is his acknowledgment of the primitive, the infantile, the unreconstructed libidinous in himself, but it is not merely or only a general, mandatory Christian humility confessing to the frailties of the worser self that speaks in

And my ending is despair,
Unless I be relieved by prayer,
Which pierces so, that it assaults
Mercy itself, and frees all faults.

Prospero's melancholy at the end of his immense effort to conquer and to sublimate is perhaps, at one very realistic level, no more than the collapse into depression of the euphoric, creatively imaginative moment. But I think we read the play's fantasy more fully if we read in it more than a reflex lassitude. It is the wound of Narcissus, the pain both of renunciation itself and of the knowledge of the dark backward and abysm of love. Every man is an island, or an ark, severed from its continent, doomed to lack what is most loved, to sail nowhere but to death.

The Tempest is therefore Shakespeare's most indissolubly tragicomic drama. Prospero's restitutive project – "to please" – was of the highest human value. For its success the "gentle breath" of audience empathy, the clapping of their – our – "good hands" is required. But the liberation for which Prospero begs the audience's "indulgence" is the freedom, now that all is over, to mourn.

Notes

CHAPTER 1   BEYOND GENRE

1. See Marvin T. Herrick, *Tragicomedy: Its Origin and Development in Italy, France and England* (Urbana, Illinois University Press, 1955) and Colie (1974).
2. *All's Well* has mostly been perceived as a "dark" comedy (possibly because of the sexual anxieties implicit in its story), and it shares with *Measure for Measure* the use of the counterphobic bed-trick, but overall I think it is best seen as a deeper, more probing variant within the earlier group of festive maturation comedies than as a precursor tragicomedy.
3. Quoted from "Ode to Himself," which was written after the failure of his play, *The New Inn* (1629).
4. See Tzvetan Todorov, *The Fantastic*, trans. Richard Howard (Ithaca, Cornell University Press, 1975) for a structuralist analysis of the genre, and Jean Bellamin-Noel, *Vers l'inconscient du texte* (Paris, Presses Universitaires de France, 1979) for a Lacanian approach.
5. Northrop Frye's account of the mode in *The Anatomy of Criticism* (New York, Atheneum, 1966) is perhaps the most comprehensive we have.
6. An exhaustive bibliography of studies of the romances is given in Kay and Jacobs (1978), and of the problem comedies in Richard P. Wheeler's *Shakespeare's Development and the Problem Comedies* (Berkeley, University of California Press, 1981).

7. The title of a paper given as the Freud Lecture at Yale, 1984.

8. See Donald Spence, *Narrative and Historical Truth: Meaning and Interpretation in Psychoanalysis* (New York, Norton, 1982).

9. Richard P. Wheeler's psychoanalytically oriented study, *Shakespeare's Development and the Problem Comedies*, is an admirable attempt at such a synthesis, as was in its day J.I.M. Stewart's *Character and Motive in Shakespeare* (London, Longman, 1949).

10. See also Terry Eagleton, *Literary Theory* (Oxford, Blackwell, 1983).

11. Norman Holland, "Literary Interpretation and Three Phases of Psychoanalysis," *Critical Inquiry*, 3 (1976), and see also "Dr Johnson's Remarks on Cordelia's Death," G. Hartman (ed.) (1978). These phases of psychoanalysis are all, as Shafer (1976) demonstrates, tainted by the reifications and spatializations of Freudian metapsychology. Shafer proposes and foresees a "fourth phase" in which a truly secondary process language describing action and behaviour will take the place of the metaphorical inner objects, places, spaces and substances still used in psychoanalytic discourse.

12. See Heinz Kohut, *The Analysis of the Self* (New York, International Universities Press, 1971). See also Margaret S. Mahler, *On Human Symbiosis and the Vicissitudes of Individuation* (New York, International Universities Press, 1968). An excellent application of Kohutian theory to poetry is to be found in David Lynch, *The Poetics of the Self* (Chicago, University of Chicago Press, 1979).

13. Francis Baudry quotes Doubrovsky's valuable caveat concerning the notion of stratification: "the profundity of a work must . . . be understood in a perceptual sense as one speaks of the depth of a visual field in which the multiplication of viewpoints can never exhaust the material to be perceived. . . . there are indeed 'depths' of meaning but not strata" (1984, 564).

14. See "The function and field of speech and language in psychoanalysis," *Ecrits* (1977, 30–113).

15. This formulation of the "key signifiers" is Paul Ricoeur's, in *The Conflict of Interpretations* (Evanston, Northwestern University Press, 1974), 109. Lacan says, "there are thousands of symbols in the sense that the term is understood in analysis, all of them refer to one's own body, to kinship relations, to birth, to life and to death" (1977, 822).

16. Quotations from Bellamin-Noel are from Jerry Aline Flieger's review, "Trial and Error: The Case of the Textual Unconscious," *Diacritics*, 11, 1981. For another use of the term, "textual unconscious" see Jonathan Culler, "Textual Self-Consciousness

and the Textual Unconscious," *Style*, 18, 3, 1984. He refers to the transferential repetition, in the interpreting reader, of the dramas the text has displayed.

17. I am indebted to Bennet Simon for this formulation of the spectrum.

CHAPTER 2   THE PERILS OF PERICLES

1. Quoted by Meredith Skura, "Interpreting Posthumus' Dream From Above and Below: Families, Psychoanalysts, and Literary Critics," in Schwartz and Kahn (1980, 204).

2. P. Goolden, "Antioch's Riddle in Gower and Shakespeare," *Review of English Studies*, n.s. VI, 23 (1955), 251, reviews the history of the riddle from the Latin prose *Apollonius*, where involuted in-law relations provide the clues, through Gower's Middle English version to Shakespeare's adaptation in *Pericles*. He notes that Shakespeare's innovation allows for simplification; he ignores, however, the oddity that catches our attention. R.E. Gajdusek, "Death, Incest and the Triple Bond," *American Imago* 31, 2 (1974), 109–30 has recourse to a Jungian Triple Goddess both for the riddle and the play which he reads as a mythical contest between the feminine (all-devouring) and the masculine (separative) principles. Dr Rivka Eifferman, in the course of a seminar on Psychoanalysis and Literature held at the *Hebrew University Centre for Literary Studies* in 1985, suggests the possibility that "All love the womb that their first being bred" could paraphrase as "All love the daugther that they first (in their youth) raised," thus providing a literal solution to the riddle and obviating recourse to the unconscious.

3. The riddle contains metalepsis in Quintillian's sense: the metonymical substitution of one word for another which is itself figurative. But I am using the term in the sense made familiar in narratology: transpositions of past and present, foreboding and retrospection. Both senses offer paradigms for the psychoanalytic process.

4. For an account of levels of representation in Shakespeare – the use of choric figures, plays-within-plays, actors acting actors, on-stage audiences and other parabastic devices, see Aviva Furdi, "The Play with a Play Within the Play," Ph.D. dissertation, Hebrew University (1984). See also the interesting earlier account of "multi-consciousness" given by S.L. Bethell, *Shakespeare and the Popular Dramatic Tradition* (London, King & Staples, 1944).

5. In a recent article, "The Idea of a Psychoanalytical Literary Criticism," to be published in *Critical Inquiry*.

6. See Arden edn for an account of the textual problems in this passage. I am indebted to Dr Rivka Eifferman for the primal scene insight.

7. Alan B. Rothenberg, "Infantile Fantasies in Shakespearean Metaphor," *Psychoanalytic Review*, 60, 2 (1973), 215, notices the image of maternal devouring in I.v.41–3, and points out that in the 1609 and 1611 Q texts of *Pericles* "nousle" (to nurse) is spelled "nouzell" (our nuzzle – to thrust the nose into). The composite neatly condenses feeding and projective threat, mother and child.

8. *The Comedy of Errors*, derived from the same literary source as *Pericles* – the popular fifth-century *Apollonius of Tyre* – is evidently a younger oedipal fantasy in which the threatened father, Egeus, is rescued by his son. See Freud on rescue fantasies in "Family Romance" (1909).

9. In A. Norman Jeffares, *A Commentary on the Collected Poems of W.B. Yeats* (Stanford University Press, 1968), 66; and *The Variorum Edition of the Plays of W.B. Yeats*, ed. R.K. Alspach (London, Macmillan, 1966), 571.

10. Norman Nathan noticed the Jonah connection, *Notes and Queries*, Jan. 1956, 10–11.

11. David Willbern pursues the symbolism of circles, zeros and O's in "Shakespeare's Nothing," (in Schwartz and Kahn, 1980), 244–64.

12. I am grateful to Dr Paul Gabriner for suggesting this onomastic possibility.

13. This difficult line has been glossed in many ways. The 1609 Q text has "not," which is followed by F.D. Hoeniger's Arden edn (London, Methuen, 1963), and by Ernest Schanzer in the Signet (New York, New American Library, 1965). Philip Edwards' emendation in the New Penguin edn (Harmondsworth, Penguin, 1976) is "but," which makes good sense for the reading here advanced. Edwards suggests that the aside be given to Thaisa, which however would destroy the repartee effect of her "Juno" to Simonides' "Jove."

14. See Gaston Bachelard, *The Poetics of Space*, trans. Maria Jolas (Boston, Beacon Press, 1964), Ch. 5, for an interesting discussion of the symbolism of shells.

15. As Robert Rogers says, "Whenever decomposition (splitting, doubling or multiplication of personae) takes place in narrative, the cast of characters is never quite as large as it would appear to be" (1970, 63).

16. In *Comic Transformations in Shakespeare* (London, Methuen, 1980), I have attempted to develop a cathartic, or "exorcist" theory of comic form.

CHAPTER 3 *CYMBELINE:* THE RESCUE OF THE KING

1. Bertrand Evans, *Shakespeare's Comedies* (Oxford, Clarendon Press, 1960), has shown how the discrepancy between audience knowledge and character knowledge is greater in *Cymbeline* than in any other of Shakespeare's plays. The characters are kept more ignorant and of more essential matters than anywhere else. Hence the accumulation of discoveries in Act V.
2. See Gilbert D. Chaitin, "The Representation of Logical Relations in Dreams and the Nature of Primary Process," *Psychoanalysis and Contemporary Thought*, II (1978); Pinchas Noy, "A Revision of the Psychoanalytic Theory of Primary Process," *Int. Jnl. Psycho-Analysis*, 50 (1969); and "Symbolism and Mental Representation," *Annual of Psychoanalysis*, I (1973) for useful accounts of primary and secondary processes of thought.
3. Most famous of the Victorian adorers is Swinburne who calls Imogen "the very crown and flower of all her father's daughters . . . woman above all Shakespeare's women . . . the immortal godhead of womanhood" (*A Study of Shakespeare*, 1880).
4. See Richard Levin, *The Multiple Plot in English Renaissance Drama* (Chicago, University of Chicago Press, 1971).
5. In general Schwartz' rigorously "Applied Psychoanalysis" is only partially successful. It suffers from an excessive orthodoxy which attempts to diagnose and schematize exhaustively in accordance with classic psychoanalytic terms and themes. And he tends to see Imogen exclusively as an object of the men's fantasies. "Shakespeare," he says, "forces Imogen to reenact regressive states we see in Cymbeline and Posthumus. . . . In this inverted primal scene Imogen is the "man" who "dies" at the sight of the castrated body; she has become a surrogate for Posthumus, who is "killed" by the sight of the female genitals. The scene works to deny the masculine fantasy by expressing it in an utterly inverted way" (266).
6. See Ruth Nevo, *Comic Transformations in Shakespeare* (London, Methuen, 1980).
7. Cf. in *Measure for Measure*, IV.ii.1–5 and *Romeo and Juliet*, I.i.21–6.
8. Discussion of the problem and its implications for the question of authorship can be found in Nosworthy (1980, xxxvi–vii).
9. The omission may seem less surprising when one recalls that the Three Caskets essay (1913) does antedate by many years the loving care bestowed upon her ailing father by his "Anna-Antigone," as Freud called his own beloved daughter. See *Letters of Sigmund Freud, 1873–1939*, ed. Tania Stern and James Stern (New York, Basic Books, 1960), 424.

10. The phrase is Freud's in *Creative Writers and Daydreaming* (1908).

CHAPTER 4   DELUSIONS AND DREAMS: *THE WINTER'S TALE*

1. For confusion about his role see Lee Sheridan Cox, "The role of Autolycus in *The Winter's Tale*," *Studies in English Literature*, 9 (1969) 287, and passim.
2. Nevill Coghill, "Six Points of Stage-Craft in *The Winter's Tale*," *Sh.Survey* (1958) introduced his defence of the play with the statement: "It is a critical commonplace that *The Winter's Tale* is an ill-made play: its very editors deride it" (31). How far the balance had been redressed by 1978 may be judged by Charles Frey's judgement in "Tragic Structure in The Winter's Tale": "*The Winter's Tale* carries its often painful but always instructive burden extremely well" (Kay and Jacobs, 1978, 124).
3. See Louise George Clubb, "Shakespeare's Comedy and Late Cinquecento Mixed Genres" in *Shakespearean Comedy*, ed. M. Charney (New York, New York Literary Forum, 1980).
4. Psychoanalytically minded critics have pounced upon the "twinned lambs" speech as upon a treasure trove for explication. J.I.M. Stewart, *Character and Motive in Shakespeare* (1948) was the first to find a displaced return of repressed homosexuality in Leontes' obsessional outburst, and W.H. Auden ("The Alienated City," *Encounter*, 1961) was convinced that "Leontes is a classic case of paranoid sexual jealousy due to repressed homosexual feelings" (11). Stephen Reid, "*The Winter's Tale*" (*American Imago* 27 (1970)) and Murray Schwartz, "Leontes' Jealousy in *The Winter's Tale*" (*American Imago* 30 (1973)) and "*The Winter's Tale*: Loss and Transformation" (*American Imago* 32 (1975)), proceed from Freud's formula for defensive projection ("I do not love him. She does") to further analytical variations on the theme of delusional jealousy. These critics provide a clinical diagnosis for a sudden seizure like Leontes'; what they do not do is to provide an entry into the play. They lead out of the drama, not into it. Their phantasmagoric choreography of Kleinean projections and introjections is unlikely to be available to readers and audiences, even those most closely attuned to the vagaries of primary process; and they produce a distinct impression of overkill. There is a danger in overexplication; the danger, as J-B. Pontalis aptly puts it in a corrective essay, "of strangling the eloquence of oneiric life" ("Dream as an Object," *Int. Rev. of Psychoanalysis*, 1974, 1).

5. For a useful account of the two principles of mental functioning see Pinchas Noy (1979), 185 and passim. See also Robert Rogers (1978). Carol Thomas Neely, *"The Winter's Tale*: The Triumph of Speech," *Studies in English Literature*, 15 (1975) gives an account of the speech in terms of the rationalistic language of euphuism and the "indeterminate" language of passion.

6. See the Arden edn, (London, Methuen, 1963) for extended commentary on the speech. Older commentary extends to three pages (27–30) in the Variorum.

7. Wallace Stevens, "An Ordinary Evening in New Haven," xxviii, *The Palm at the End of the Mind* (New York, Vintage, 1972), 349.

8. David Willbern, "Shakespeare's Nothing" (Schwartz and Kahn, 1980) gives an illuminating exposition of the imagery of Shakespeare's "dialectic of nothing and all" (252). See also Antoinette Dauber, "This Great Gap of Time," *Hebrew University Studies in Literature and the Arts*, 11, 2 (1983) for an excellent reading of the play along similar lines.

9. See Freud, "Revision of Dream Theory," *New Introductory Lectures* (1933) 53.

10. OED gives 1604 for the first usage of the term; the sense was "to deceive or blind." The word occurs nowhere in Shakespeare.

11. I am much indebted to discussion with Stanley Cavell for insight into this manifestation of the textual unconscious.

CHAPTER 5   SUBTLETIES OF THE ISLE: *THE TEMPEST*

The lines from "An Ordinary Evening in New Haven" by Wallace Stevens are reprinted from *The Collected Poems of Wallace Stevens* by permission of Alfred A. Knopf, Inc. and Faber and Faber Ltd.

1. On the philosophy of magic as a discipline of the soul see Kermode (1962) xviii.

2. Ludwig Jekels, "On the Psychology of Comedy," *Imago*, XII (1926) develops the notion of courtship comedy as essentially oedipal from the son's point of view.

3. Kermode (1962, 18) points out how "the imagery of Prospero suddenly changes," becoming conceited and Italianate ("To cry to th'sea that roar'd to us; to sigh/To th'winds, whose pity, sighing back again,/Did us but loving wrong" (I.ii.149–51), when, in the dialogue with Miranda, he shifts from "reality," the level of the "probable and natural," to the level of the "miraculous."

4. The genitive "of," always ambiguously indicative of part or whole, makes "the dark backward and abysm" either the whole

passage of time itself, or some part or aspect of time, ie. the inevitable loss of memory caused by the passage of time.

5. K.M. Abenheimer, "Shakespeare's *Tempest*, A Psychological Analysis," *Psychoanalytic Review*, 33 (1946), rptd in Faber (1970), takes this Jungian view, but he sees the play as a dramatic representation of Prospero's failure to overcome "inflated loneliness, paranoid isolation" and "archaic and magical fantasies about women as either horrible witches or Mirandas" (1970, 515). Such a reading fails to take into account Prospero's manifest successes. One would have thought that Prospero's acceptance of his "shadow," Caliban, would have met with the approval of a Jungian.

6. Among others, Theodore Reik, *Fragment of a Great Confession* (New York, Farrar Straus & Co, 1949); Leo Lowenthal, *Literature and the Image of Man* (Boston, Beacon Press, 1957); Charles K. Hofling, "Psychological Aspects of Shakespeare's *Tempest*," *Psychoanalytic Review*, 61 (1974); and Morton Kaplan and Robert Kloss, *The Unspoken Motive* (New York, The Free Press, 1973).

7. On the complex Renaissance conceptions of nature see Kermode, Arden edn. (1958), xxxiv–xliii.

8. See Richard Levin, *The Multiple Plot in English Renaissance Drama* (Chicago, Chicago University Press, 1971).

9. See Erwin Panofsky, *Studies in Iconology* (New York, Harper & Row, 1962), 74. Jeffrey Mehlman refers to this iconology in his discussion of the Lacanian emphasis upon the notion of the fragile narcissistic ego as opposed to the Freudian ego, agent of synthesis, mastery, integration, and adaptation. See "The 'floating signifier': from Levi-Strauss to Lacan," *Yale French Studies*, 48 (1972).

References

All citations from the works of Shakespeare are from the *Riverside Edition*, ed. G. Blakemore Evans (Boston, Houghton Mifflin, 1974). For quotations from Freud I have used wherever possible the Pelican Freud Library, based on the *Standard Edition*, ed. James Strachey and Angela Richards (Harmondsworth, 1976–).

Arlow, Jacob A. (1979) "Metaphor and the Psychoanalytic Situation," *Psychoanalytic Qu.*, XLVIII.

Barber, C.L. (1969) "'Thou that beget'st him that did thee beget': Transformation in *Pericles* and *The Winter's Tale*," *Shakespare Survey*, 22.

Barker, G.A. (1963) "Themes and Variations in *Pericles*," English Studies, 41.

Barton, Anne (ed.) (1980) *The Tempest*, New Penguin edn (Harmondsworth, Penguin).

Baudry, Francis (1984) "An Essay on Method in Applied Psychoanalysis," *Psychoanalytic Qu.*, LIII.

Bettelheim, Bruno (1976) *The Uses of Enchantment* (London, Thames & Hudson).

Bloom, Harold (1975) *A Map of Misreading* (Oxford University Press). (1976) *Poetry & Repression* (New Haven, Yale University Press).

Brooks, Peter (1980) "Repetition, Repression, and Return," *New Literary History*.

Colie, Rosalie (1974) *Shakespeare's Living Art* (New Jersey, Princeton University Press).

Eagleton, Terry (1983) *Literary Theory* (Oxford, Blackwell).

Edwards, Philip (1958) "Shakespeare's Romances: 1900–1957, *Shakespeare Survey*, 11.

(Ed.) 1976, *Pericles* (Harmondsworth, Penguin).

Ehrenzveig, Anton (1967) *The Hidden Order of Art* (Berkeley, University of California Press).

Faber, M.D. (ed.) (1970) *The Design Within* (New York, Science House).

Felman, Shoshana (1978) "Turning the Screw of Interpretation," *Psychoanalysis and Literature, Yale French Studies*, 55/56.

(1980) "On Reading Poetry: Reflections on the Limits and Possibilities of Psychoanalytic Approaches," in *The Literary Freud*, ed. J.H. Smith, *Psychiatry and the Humanities*, 4 (New Haven, Yale University Press).

(1980/1) "The Originality of Jaques Lacan," *Poetics Today* 2, 1b.

Foakes, R.A. (1971) *Shakespeare: The Dark Comedies to the Last Plays* (London, Routledge & Kegan Paul).

Freud, Sigmund (1900) *The Interpretation of Dreams* (*PFL*, 4).

(1901) *The Psychopathology of Everyday Life* (*PFL*, 5).

(1905) *Jokes and their Relation to the Unconscious* (*PFL*, 6).

([1906] 1956) *Delusion and Dream (1906) and Other Essays*, ed. Philip Rieff (Boston, Beacon Press).

(1909) "Creative Writers and Daydreaming" (*SE*, IX).

(1911) "Formulations on the Two Principles of Mental Functioning" (*PFL*, 11).

(1915–16) *Introductory Lectures (SE*, XV).

(1915–17) "Mourning and Melancholia" (*PFL*, 11).

(1920) "Beyond the Pleasure Principle" (*PFL*, 11).

(1923) *The Ego and the Id* (*PFL*, 11).

(1933) *New Introductory Lectures* (*PFL*, 2).

(1938) "The Splitting of the Ego in the Process of Defence" (*PFL*, 11).

Frye, Northrop (1959) Introduction, *The Tempest* (Harmondsworth, Penguin).

([1963] 1971) *Fables of Identity*, in *Shakespeare's Later Comedies*, ed. D.J. Palmer, (Harmondsworth, Penguin).

Garber, Marjorie B. (1974) *Dreams in Shakespeare: From Metaphor to Metamorphosis*, (New Haven, Yale University Press).

Gordon, David J. (1980) "Literature and Repression: The Case of Shavian Drama," in *The Literary Freud*, ed. J.H. Smith (New Haven, Yale University Press).

Green, André (1978) "The Double and the Absent," in *Psychoanalysis, Creativity and Literature*, ed. Alan Roland (New York,

Columbia University Press).

(1979) *The Tragic Effect: The Oedipus Complex in Tragedy*, trans. Alan Sheridan (Cambridge University Press).

(1985) "The Unbinding Process," *NLH*.

Hartman, Geoffrey (ed.) (1978) *Psychoanalysis and the Question of the Text* (Baltimore, Johns Hopkins University Press).

Hartwig, Joan, (1978) "The Tragicomic Perspective of *The Winter's Tale*," *English Literary History*.

Hoeniger, F.D. (1976) "Shakespeare's Romances," *Shakespeare Survey*, 29.

(Ed.) (1963) *Pericles* (London, Methuen).

Hofling, Charles K. (1965) "Notes on Shakespeare's *Cymbeline*," *Shakespeare Studies*.

(1974) "Psychological Aspects of Shakespeare's *Tempest*," *Psychoanalytic Review*, 61.

Holland, Norman (1964) *Psychoanalysis and Shakespeare* (New York, McGraw-Hill).

(1968) *The Dynamics of Literary Response*, (New York, Oxford University Press).

([1968] 1970) "Caliban's Dream," *Psychoanalytical Quarterly*, XXXVII. Reptd in *The Design Within*, ed. M.D. Faber (New York, Science House).

(1976) "Literary Interpretation and Three Phases of Psychoanalysis," *Critical Inquiry*, 3.

Hoy, Cyrus (1978) "Fathers and Daughters in Shakespeare's Romances," in *Shakespeare's Romances Reconsidered*, ed. Carol McGinnis Kay and Henry E. Jacobs (Lincoln, University of Nebraska Press).

James, D.J. (1937) *Scepticism and Poetry* (London, Allen & Unwin).

Johnson, S. (1958) *Yale Edition of the Work of Samuel Johnson*, ed. W.J. Bates and A.B. Strauss (New Haven, Yale University Press).

Jones, Ernest ([1923] 1955) *Hamlet and Oedipus* (New York, Doubleday).

Kahn, Coppelia (1980) "The Providential Tempest and the Shakespearean Family," in *Representing Shakespeare*, ed. Murray M. Schwartz and Coppelia Kahn (Baltimore, Johns Hopkins University Press).

Kaufman, R.J. (1963) "Puzzling Epiphanies," *Essays in Criticism*, 13.

Kay, Carol McGinnis and Jacobs, Henry E. (1978) *Shakespeare's Romances Reconsidered* (Lincoln, University of Nebraska Press).

Kermode, Frank (ed.) (1958) *The Tempest*, Arden edn (London, Methuen).

Knight, G. Wilson (1930) *The Wheel of Fire* (London).

Knights, L.C. (1946) *Explorations* (London, Chatto & Windus).

Kris, Ernst and Gombrich, E.H. (1964) *Psychoanalytic Explorations in*

164   *Shakespeare's Other Language*

Art (New York, Schocken).

Kris, Ernst (1956) "On Some Vicissitudes of Insight in Psycho-analysis," *Int.Jnl of Psychoanalysis*, 37.

Kristeva, Julia (1980) *Desire in Language* (New York, Columbia University Press).

Lacan, Jaques ([1966] 1977) *Ecrits*, trans. Alan Sheridan (New York, Norton).

(1972) "The Seminar on *The Purloined Letter*," trans. J. Mehlman, *Yale French Studies* 48.

Lanham, Richard (1968) *A Handlist of Rhetorical Terms* (Berkeley, University of California Press).

Lawlor, J. (1962) "Pandosto and the Nature of Dramatic Romance," *Philological Quarterly*, 41.

Lesser, Simon (1957) *Fiction and the Unconscious* (Chicago, Chicago University Press).

Mahood, M. ([1957] 1971) *Shakespeare's Word Play* (London, Methuen), and in *Shakespeare's Later Comedies*, ed. D.J. Palmer (Harmondsworth, Penguin).

Matchett, William H. (1969) "Some Dramatic Techniques in *The Winter's Tale*," *Shakespeare Survey*, 22.

Mowatt, Barbara A. (1976) *The Dramaturgy of Shakespeare's Romances* (Athens, University of Georgia Press).

Nosworthy, J.M. (ed.) (1980) *Cymbeline* (London, Methuen).

Noy, Pinchas (1979) "Analytic Theory of Cognitive Development," *The Psychoanalytical Study of the Child*, 34.

Palmer, D.J. (1971) *Shakespeare's Later Comedies* (Harmondsworth, Penguin).

Richards, I.A. (1968) *Coleridge on Imagination* (London, Routledge & Kegan Paul).

Ricoeur, Paul (1970) *Freud and Philosophy: An Essay in Interpretation* (New Haven, Yale University Press).

(1974) *The Conflict of Interpretations* (Evanston, Northwestern University Press).

Rogers, Robert (1970) *A Psychoanalytical Study of the Double in Literature* (Detroit, Wayne State University Press).

(1978) *Metaphor: A Psycholoanalytical View* (Berkeley, University of California Press).

Roland, Alan (ed.) (1978) *Psychoanalysis, Creativity and Literature* (New York, Columbia University Press).

(1978) "Toward a Reorientation of Psychoanalytical Literary Criticism," in *Psychoanalysis, Creativity and Literature*, ed. Alan Roland (New York, Columbia University Press).

Rorty, Amelie (ed.) (1976) *The Identities of Persons* (Berkeley, University of California Press).

Schafer, Roy (1976) *A New Language for Psychoanalysis* (New Haven,

Yale University Press).

Schanzer, Ernest (ed.) (1965) *Pericles* (New York, New American Library).

(Ed.) (1969) *The Winter's Tale* (Harmondsworth, Penguin).

Schwartz, Murray M. (1976) "Between Fantasy and Imagination," in *The Practice of Psychoanalytic Criticism*, ed. L. Tennenhouse (Detroit, Wayne State University Press).

Schwartz, Murray M. and Kahn, Coppelia (eds) (1980) *Representing Shakespeare* (Baltimore, Johns Hopkins University Press).

Siemon, James Edward (1974) " 'But it Appears She Lives': Iteration in *The Winter's Tale*," *PMLA*, 74.

Skura, Meredith (1980) "Revisions and Rereadings in Dreams and Allegories," in *The Literary Freud*, ed. J.H. Smith (New Haven, Yale University Press).

(1981) *The Literary Use of the Psychoanalytic Process* (New Haven, Yale University Press).

(1986) "Interpreting Posthumus' Dream from Above and Below: Families, Psychoanalysis, and Literary Critics," in *Representing Shakespeare*, ed. Murray M. Schwartz, and Coppelia Kahn (Baltimore, Johns Hopkins University Press).

Strachey, Lytton (1922) *Books and Characters* (London, Chatto & Windus).

Taine, Hippolyte ([1863] 1871) *History of English Literature*, trans. H. von Laun (London, Chatto & Windus).

Tillyard, E.M.W. (1938) *Shakespeare's Last Plays* (London, Chatto & Windus).

Traversi, Derek (1969) *An Approach to Shakespeare* (New York, Doubleday Anchor) 3rd edn.

(1965) *Shakespeare's Last Phase* (Stanford, Stanford University Press).

Trilling, Lionel (1951) *The Liberal Imagination* (New York, Viking).

Winnicott, D.W. (1974) "Fear of Breakdown," *Int. Rev. of Psychoanalysis.*

Wright, Elizabeth (1984) *Psychoanalytic Criticism* (London, Methuen).

Index